22.95

1947

1947
A Memoir of Indian Independence

By

M. Zahir

Order this book online at www.trafford.com
or email orders@trafford.com

Most Trafford titles are also available at major online book retailers.

● Copyright 2009, 2010 M. Zahir.

All rights reserved. No part of this publication may be reproduced, stored in a retrieval system, or transmitted, in any form or by any means, electronic, mechanical, photocopying, recording, or otherwise, without the written prior permission of the author.

Printed in the United States of America.

ISBN: 978-1-4269-1501-7 (sc)

Trafford rev. 11/15/2010

 www.trafford.com

North America & international
toll-free: 1 888 232 4444 (USA & Canada)
phone: 250 383 6864 ♦ fax: 812 355 4082

India won its Independence from the British on August 14, 1947. Within a few months, an ancient and stable multicultural society lay in tatters, with close to two million innocent people dead, either murdered or dead of disease and starvation. Nobody has ever been charged for this mind-numbing calamity.

I was ten years old then. This is the story of events as I witnessed, leading to and following the Independence.

I am deeply grateful to my brother Rafiq who is the only other living survivor of our family from 1947. His phenomenal memory has filled many gaps.

Victoria, Canada, 2009
mzahir1947@gmx.com

To
Dharam Pal, naturally

CONTENTS

Prologue	xi
The Catastrophe	75
Epilogue	101
Notes	131
Glossary	137
Selected Reading	145

PROLOGUE

India will be divided over my dead body.
Gandhi

I will have India divided or India destroyed.
Jinnah

1

I HAD NOT done my homework that day.
The day before, I had started to feel sick at school, though I had managed to get through the day. Returning home, I told my mother I was unwell.

"You lie down and get some rest," she said. "And don't go out and play with Amrit this evening." Amrit Lal was my friend and neighbour.

"What would you like to eat?" she asked.

"I am not hungry," I replied.

"You should eat something. Why don't I soak some *chapatis* in *shorba* and you have it with a glass of milk?

"All right," I said unenthusiastically. "I have homework to do, too. Master Gill has asked us to write *paharas* on the *takhti*."

"Well," said my mother, "just tell him tomorrow you were not well. Perhaps you should take the day off tomorrow."

I said nothing. I knew that Master Gill did not believe what students said. Perhaps he was right. The students were always making excuses. How could he tell who was telling the truth?

I ate *chapatis* soaked in *shorba*, drank some warm milk, and lay down. When my father came, my mother told him I was not well. My father touched my forehead.

"I don't think he has a fever. Let him rest," he said.

We lived in a small town called Mukerian in the Punjab province of India. Mukerian was then at the end of a railway line, a branch line from Jalandhar. My father was in charge of the small government hospital there. We lived in the hospital compound in a house provided by the government. At that time we were only five people in the house, my father, my mother, my brother Rafiq who was four years older than I, and my eldest sister, Hamida, who had been taken out of school to help my mother with the chores at home as my mother was not in good health. My two other sisters, Majida and Rashida, and one brother, Bashir, were away at the college while my oldest brother, Sadiq, after finishing medical school in Amritsar, had joined the Indian Army and was somewhere in Southeast Asia. My father was assisted by three *compounders* and a nurse. One of the *compounders*, Pandit Bansi Lal, my friend Amrit's father, lived next door, the other two lived in town. The nurse, Miss Daniel, lived next to Bansi Lal. The hospital also employed a number of servants who lived in the servants' quarters on the other side of the hospital.

The school Rafiq and I attended was called Anglo-Sanskrit High School (A.S. High School). It was a government school and had classes from grade 1 to grade 10. I don't know why the word "Sanskrit" was used in the school's name as no Sanskrit was taught in the school.

The following morning I felt reasonably well and decided to go to school. I was a conscientious student and hardly ever missed school.

The second class in the morning was Master Gill's. As expected, he asked us to show our homework. His routine was to call each student one by one to the front, where he sat behind a table checking the homework. Anyone who had not done his homework was asked to stand on his left side facing the class.

That morning there were four of us who had not done their homework and so we stood there facing the class.

"Why have you not done your homework?" he asked each of us.

"Sir, I was not feeling well," I answered truthfully.

He did not believe any of us. "You don't look sick," he said to me.

He then squeezed our ears, one of the standard methods of punishment, and then ordered us back to our seats.

By now I was feeling awful. As soon as the class was over, I picked up my *basta* and started walking home. The moment I reached home, I went into my mother's arms and started sobbing. She immediately spread a *durrie* on a *charpoy* and made me lie down and covered me with a blanket. It was early winter and fairly cold.

"Your father should be home for lunch soon," she said as she stroked my head. "In the meantime you should drink some water." She asked Hamida to heat a little water in a cup on the coals in the *chulla* and bring it to me. My mother believed that a sick person, in cool weather, should drink warm water. I drank the tepid water while my mother sat by my side massaging my head.

When my father came home, he touched my forehead. "He is a little feverish, I think," he said. He took out the thermometer from his pocket, removed it from its metal case, shook the mercury down and put it in my mouth. After a minute or so he took it out.

"101 degrees. Malaria, I suppose, though the malaria season should be over. Let us give him some quinine."

I knew the routine. I had been through it many times. Whenever anyone in the family felt unwell and became feverish, quinine pills were doled out. They were so bitter! My mother stood by my side as I put each pill as far back in my throat as possible and immediately swallowed it with some water.

In the evening my mother made some *dalia* for me, as I was still sick and had vomited a few more times.

The following day I felt even worse and had aches and pains all over. The course of quinine was continued. After three or four days I was still running a temperature and feeling weaker by the day. A fever from malaria should have broken by now.

It was then that I heard the dreaded word, 'typhoid'. My father was now becoming convinced that I had typhoid. There was no laboratory in the hospital; if the fever did not respond to quinine the diagnosis was changed from malaria to typhoid. My diet was now changed drastically. All solid food was prohibited; it was now only water and milk, with occasional Horlicks or Ovaltine.

My condition nonetheless continued to deteriorate. Hamida sat by me for hours, quietly praying and reading

Quran. Hamida was very religious, and was the only one in our family who prayed five times a day. Miss Daniel came to visit me daily. She sat down on a chair by my bed and said some encouraging words. Once or twice she brought a book and read it to me. I cannot remember what book it was, perhaps the Bible, as Miss Daniel was Christian. Amrit came every day after school and told me all the school news. Pandit Bansi Lal came too, and said something sacred in Hindi or Sanskrit.

It was about this time, when my condition had really deteriorated and my family was beginning to despair, that someone suggested to my mother that we should call Maulvi Azhar to say special prayers at my bedside. Maulvi Azhar was the *mullah* at the city mosque. He was a well respected man. Apart from looking after the mosque and leading prayers, he ran a small orphanage. Rafiq had occasionally taken me to the mosque on Fridays, and I had heard Maulvi Azhar's Friday sermons. The sermons were generally about the importance of saying prayers, fasting in Ramadan, and giving *zakat*. Occasionally, he told the story of some miracle which he had witnessed or taken part in. The one I remember was when Maulvi Azhar was travelling in a bus and the bus broke down. The driver tried everything but could not start the engine. It was very hot and they were in the middle of nowhere. Maulvi Azhar stepped down from the bus, stood by the engine, recited Quran and blew towards the engine. He then asked the driver to start the bus. The engine fired and the bus was on its way. Whenever Maulvi Azhar told a stunning tale like that, the people quietly murmured *Allah o Akbar*.

My father was not keen on the idea of inviting Maulvi Azhar. My father never went to the mosque, though he knew Maulvi Sahib well as he often visited the orphanage to treat sick orphans. Maulvi Sahib was always very grateful to my father but my father avoided meeting him because my father was embarrassed about not going to the mosque. Hamida thought inviting Maulvi Sahib was a great idea. So my father gave in and sent his friend, Ramzan Ali, to see if Maulvi Sahib would be willing to come. Maulvi Sahib not only agreed but accompanied Ramzan right away to our house.

Maulvi Azhar was over six feet tall, had a flowing white beard, and wore a large white turban. He looked very impressive. He stood by my bed with my father, Rafiq, and Ramzan Ali, and loudly recited verses from the Quran. At the end he said "amen" and everyone else said "amen." He then looked at my father and said softly, "It would help if we could sprinkle some *Abe Zamzam* on the boy."

We all knew about *Abe Zamzam*. All Muslims do. *Zamzam* is an ancient spring in Mecca. Muslims believe that Prophet Ibrahim and his wife Hajira were staying there with their infant son Ismail when they ran out of water. Ismail was very thirsty, and Hajira was desperately seeking water for her infant son. Hajira ran back and forth seven times in the scorching heat between the two hills of Safa and Marwah near Mecca, looking for water. Ismail, desperate with thirst, was hitting the ground with his heels, and suddenly, right under Ismail's heels, Allah made a spring of fresh water to appear. This was *Zamzam*. Every year, during the Hajj, Muslims drink water from this spring and often bring some back in sealed cans.

"*Abe Zamzam!*" my father said in surprise. "Where are we going to get the *Abe Zamzam*?"

"Well," Maulvi Sahib stroked his beard, "I don't know, but there might be someone in town who has recently returned from Hajj and may have some."

My father looked at Ramzan. "Do we know any Hajji who has recently returned from Mecca?"

Ramzan shook his head.

Maulvi Sahib said, "I can announce at the next Friday prayers if anyone has *Abe Zamzam* but it is only Monday today. You may not want to wait that long." After a pause he said, "You may want the *naqari* to make a *naqar* in town."

"*Naqari?*" My father was aghast.

"Why not?" said Maulvi Sahib. "Some Hajji family may have a can of it at home and may be willing to part with it for a handsome 'donation'."

Our town, like all towns, had a *naqari*. I had heard him often going round town with his drum making *naqars*. Children loved him. Occasionally, a new business starting in town used him. Even our butcher was known to use him. In the butcher's case, *naqari* was accompanied by a boy leading a couple of healthy goats which the butcher was planning to slaughter the following morning. I had heard the rumour that the butcher was not always honest. He was, so the rumour went, known to parade fat goats and then slaughter scrawny ones. The government used him to make announcements, like prohibiting the assembly of more than five people in public to prevent communal troubles, as when Gandhi announced his 'Quit India' movement.

So it was arranged. The *naqari* made the announcement in town soliciting *Abe Zamzam*. *Abe Zamzam* was to be delivered to Maulvi Azhar at the mosque as my father did not want his name announced. To everyone's delight, particularly Hamida's, a can of *Abe Zamzam* was found. It was about the size of a small sardine can. The family gathered around me when the can was punctured and water carefully sprinkled over me while Hamida read the Quran.

The following day Hamida announced that I was looking noticeably better, and a day later, even my father noticed a fall in temperature. My appetite began to improve. It took me a few weeks to recover, but I recovered fully.

Was it *Abe Zamzam* that healed me? Hamida had no doubt. I told all my school friends, who heard it with awe, especially the Muslim friends. The story quickly spread around town. I don't know what my father thought of it, but whenever someone asked him about it, he just smiled enigmatically.

Maulvi Sahib was of course delighted to add my story to his repertoire of miracles.

The final act of this story was played out many years later. I was visiting Riyadh in Saudi Arabia as a visiting physician. My Muslim colleague Ashraf offered to take me to Mecca and Medina. I was delighted. Growing up, I had heard so much about these two cities. They are at the heart of Islam. So, one weekend Ashraf and I flew to Jeddah, rented a car and drove to

Mecca on the new modern highway. Only Muslims are allowed into Mecca and, as you near Mecca, there are signs instructing non-Muslims to take the bypass. A little later, the traffic comes to a halt as each car is checked to make sure that the occupants are Muslims. The guard just looked and waved us on.

We checked into a hotel next to the *Kaaba*. It was quite late in the evening and by the time we finished dinner, Ashraf wanted to retire to his room. I decided to take a walk. I walked into the great mosque. There it was, the *Kaaba*, floodlit, covered in black, in the middle of the vast mosque. Even this late at night, a small number of people were walking around it and kissing the *Hajar al Aswad*. How often I had heard about it! I asked a caretaker the way to *Zamzam* which is now within the enlarged mosque. When I got there, it was not quite what I had imagined as a child. I had imagined *Zamzam* to be a little spring coming out of sand and flowing to a nearby oasis, with date palms and camels. It was so different, all pipes, faucets, and sinks. You can imagine the crush of humanity here during the Hajj when millions of people descend on this place to drink its water.

But it was quiet this time of the night. I sat down, closed my eyes, and went back to that day in that dusty little town in Punjab when, lying on a *charpoy*, surrounded by the family, I was sprinkled with *Zamzam* water.

I then stepped up to a faucet, poured some *Abe Zamzam* in my palm and asked, affectionately, under my breath, *"Abe Zamzam*, did you really save my life?"* There was no answer.

I lingered for a few more minutes and then quietly walked back to the hotel.

2

I have virtually no memory of my life before the fever which struck me when I was seven. It seems that the serious illness wiped out all previous memories. As for any mementoes of the times before my illness, I have none. We lost everything in 1947.

So, I may as well start with Master Goyal. He joined our school at the end of 1945. He was a young Hindu, in his late twenties. He was tall, very handsome, and so different from other teachers that he seemed like a man from another planet. Most teachers in India gravitated to teaching because they had failed in other professions. Headmaster Bhalla, for example, was an unsuccessful lawyer. But Master Goyal was born to teach. We loved him, but it was love mixed with awe. He never punished us. There was no need for it: who would have misbehaved in his presence? He forgave us if we missed our homework. Master Goyal taught English and history but it was history that he loved above all. Even now, more than sixty years later, realizing as I do the total absurdity of Master Goyal's views, I feel a frisson when I think of him. At the time, he was our promised Messiah, though not everyone thought so, certainly not Headmaster Bhalla.

It is difficult for any Indian to teach Indian history with any kind of impartiality, if indeed there is such a thing as impartial history. It is usually said that history is written by the conquerors. It is certainly true that it is written by those who have the ability to write and have the resources at hand. Indians rarely wrote their own history. The history books we used were written either by the British in India or by the Indians under British supervision. They were not as biased as the history books written by Indians and Pakistanis after Independence, but they nevertheless gave the British view of Indian history and glorified the King-Emperor. Master Goyal wanted to change all that. He wanted to tell us the 'true history' of India, and he did it with incredible panache. Master Goyal knew that in Indian culture a speaker must be emotional to be effective. Who wants to listen to dry facts, delivered without passion? Our history books were routinely divided into three periods: Hindu, Muslim, and British. Master Goyal spent much time teaching the last part of the British period, especially the Indian Independence Movement, which was then a hot subject. For the Hindu and the Muslim periods, he rarely deviated from the text. As a teacher, Master Goyal was neither a Muslim nor a Hindu, only a patriotic Indian.

The man Master Goyal admired most was Subhash Chandra Bose who had just then been declared dead in a mysterious plane crash in Formosa, present-day Taiwan, though many Indians believed he was still alive. Master Goyal called Bose, *Netaji*, 'the revered leader', and told us that, given the full support of the Indian masses, Bose would have taken India to a glorious military victory against the British. "Only if the Indians had listened to *Netaji* and supported him and not followed that weak-kneed Gandhi," Master Goyal said.

If Gandhi was a pinprick in the British side, Bose was a dagger, or at least that is what Bose wanted to be. Britain was his enemy number one. "My enemy's enemy is my friend" was his life-long motto. It was this motto which took Bose to strange places and led him to make strange friends.

Bose was born to an upper middle-class Bengali family. Like many Indian students he was devoted to scholastic studies and won scholarships to the prestigious Presidency College in Calcutta — where he assaulted a British professor for alleged racist remarks — and to Fitzsimons College at Cambridge.

On his return to India he came under the influence of Chittaranjan Das, a nationalist Bengali lawyer who, after his return to India from Britain, burnt his Western clothes and adopted homespun raiment. In 1921 Bose was first imprisoned for his revolutionary ideas, and he was in and out of prison eleven times. While in prison, Bose read extensively and formulated his views along the lines of both communism and fascism. Whenever out of prison, Bose showed remarkable organizational and oratorical skills. In 1930, Bose became the mayor of Calcutta, the largest city in India. It was natural that a man of his talents should gravitate towards politics and consequently he joined the Congress Party, the preeminent Indian political party. Bose did not believe in negotiations, *hartals, satyagrahas*, that "claptrap so dear to Gandhi" as Master Goyal put it. Bose wanted to be a man of action and, as they say of great people, a man of destiny.

In early 1930s he travelled in Europe and directly witnessed the workings of fascism and totalitarianism whose outward manifestations dazzled him. He loved the vast torchlight parades and the Nordic myths. The concentration of power at the top, the contempt for the weak, and the brain-washing propaganda of Hitler's Germany impressed him deeply. On his return to India, Bose tried to apply some of these tactics. The lazy Indian villagers, stuck in their centuries-old routine, could do with some shakeup by an Indian Gestapo officer. When Bose was elected president of the Congress Party in 1938, he staged his entrance to the meeting hall as an Indian Hitler, seated in an ancient chariot drawn by 51 white bullocks, escorted by 51 girls in saffron saris, and accompanied by 51 brass bands passing through 51 gates (51 presumably was the number of sessions planned at the meeting).

Like many Indians, Bose misunderstood Hitler and Nazis. Hitler's adoption of the ancient Hindu symbol of the swastika, his use of the term 'Aryan' and his vegetarianism flattered Indians and made them think that, unlike the British, Hitler was one of them. Whatever Hitler thought of ancient Aryans, he had nothing but contempt for modern Indians. Alfred Rosenberg, the chief ideologue of the Nazis, described Indians as "miserable bastards bathing in the dirty Ganges." Hitler in fact would have liked to strike a bargain with the British: he would give them a free hand in their Empire if they would give him a free hand in Europe.

When World War II broke out, Bose wanted to take immediate advantage of it to declare Indian independence. During one of his house arrests by the British he made his legendry escape. Dressed as Muslim *mullah*, he sneaked out of the house and reached Peshawar, a city on the border with Afghanistan. There, dressed in Afghan clothes and pretending to be a deaf-mute — for he could not speak the local language — Bose walked all the way to Kabul. In Kabul, Bose contacted the Germans and told them of his grand plan: he would help Germans defeat Britain if they would help him liberate India. The Germans in Kabul did not believe him and suspected him of being a British spy. Finally, the Italians came to his rescue. They gave him an Italian passport and an Italian name, Orlando Mazzotta. So, Mr. Mazzotta travelled to Moscow by car and train and from there flew to Berlin. His first radio broadcast from Germany caused a sensation in India as it revealed, for the first time, his whereabouts since his disappearance from his house in Calcutta.

Bose stayed in Germany for two years. His reception in Germany was less than what he had expected. He was met by low-ranking Nazi officials who let him use a radio station to air anti-British propaganda. But if Bose expected an uprising in India, he was disappointed.

Bose met Ribbentrop a couple of times but nothing much happened. Bose was as much a communist as a fascist, and his world crashed on June 22, 1941, when Germany invaded the Soviet Union. Bewildered, Bose was now trapped in Germany, at the mercy of the Germans. It was a year before he had his much anticipated meeting with Hitler. The meeting was a disaster. Hitler did almost all the talking, as was his habit. Bose asked if Hitler would make a statement in support of Indian independence. Hitler refused and told Bose that he should leave Germany and seek help from the Japanese.

Disillusioned, with the Germans facing surrender at Stalingrad, Bose took Hitler's advice and decided to try his luck with the Japanese who had overrun most of Southeast Asia and were knocking on India's door. Initial radio contact with the Japanese authorities had been positive. On February 8, 1943, Bose started his second epic journey. Germans put him in a submarine at Kiel which took him all the way around Africa where, near Madagascar, it made rendezvous with a Japanese submarine which then carried Bose to an isolated island off the coast of Indonesia from where he was flown to Japan. The Japanese showed him a little more respect than the Germans had done, and Prime Minister Tojo offered to help Bose if he would raise an army, recruited from the Indian POWs captured in Singapore and Malaya, to fight against the British. This was a heady time for Bose. There was no Hitler here to smother his ambitions and Bose could call upon the patriotic fervour of the large expatriate Indian community. Being an effective speaker and indefatigable organizer, Bose was able to form, under Japanese supervision, an 'Indian National Army' (INA) and announced the formation of the 'Provisional Government of Free India in Exile', with himself as its head of state. The Japanese, more accommodating than Hitler, recognized this government. Bose had grand plans to raise three million Indian troops, attack India through Burma, and simultaneously instigate an uprising in India. In fact, Bose could not raise, nor could Japanese arm, more than about 40,000 soldiers.

In any case, it was all too late. The Japanese were already exhausted. The high point for INA was its support of the Japanese attack on Imphal, in Northeast India, bordering Burma. Lack of air support and heavy monsoons ruined any chance of victory. The Japanese and the INA retreated, and the retreat turned into a rout through Burma, with INA and Japanese soldiers dying of disease and starvation. There was no sign of any popular uprising in India either. Bose flew to Formosa, where he was reported to have died in a plane crash on August 18, 1945. It was said that he was on his way to Russia to enlist Russia's support for yet another attack on British India. Many Indians did not believe the story of plane crash and believed that their beloved Bose would return at the head of another army for yet another struggle against the British.

Like Bose, Master Goyal had been enthralled with Hitler. I did not know then, but found out much later, that Master Goyal's habit of raising his right arm straight in front, with palm down, and saying *Jai Hind* at the end of the class was a Hitlerian imitation. After all, Master Goyal was an Aryan, like Bose and Hitler.

Master Goyal's attempts at promoting Indian independence in the classroom did not go down well with the headmaster. Headmaster Bhalla was a traditional man, and the British, after all, were still the rulers. Mr. Bhalla tried to muzzle

Master Goyal's rhetoric but Master Goyal would have none of it. It was a standoff.

Master Goyal needed a cause, a cause to challenge the headmaster. Such a cause soon appeared. We can laugh about it now, but at the time the cause almost overwhelmed the school, and even reverberated in the local community.

The war had just ended, and the restriction on kerosene oil had been slightly eased. Kerosene oil, called *miti ka tel*, was used in hurricane lanterns, though most people in the villages, and even in cities, were still using the vegetable oil in small earthen *diwas*. During the war, kerosene oil had become exceedingly scarce and was rationed. We used our lantern very sparingly for doing our homework before going to bed as you could not read by the light of a *diwa*. One morning, the headmaster announced that the authorities had sanctioned a limited amount of kerosene for the students. "The cans of kerosene will arrive next week and oil will be distributed under my supervision," announced the headmaster. Each student was asked to bring a container for his share of the oil on the day of distribution.

Here was an opportunity for Master Goyal to use his considerable oratorical skills to fight for a cause. When he came to our class the following day, he asked that the windows be closed. "Bose always planned his moves behind closed door," he said, and he then laid out the problem and the solution. The problem, according to him, was the headmaster's decision to control the distribution of kerosene. He had spoken to the headmaster, he said, and suggested that the cans of kerosene be given to the students who would then be responsible for its distribution, but the headmaster had rejected this suggestion. "How can you be sure that all the oil is distributed to you?" he asked. "Can the headmaster not keep some oil back and sell it on the black market? You know how expensive kerosene is. Is it not your oil?" he thundered.

In the next few days, before the cans were due to arrive, Master Goyal worked our class into frenzy. The plan of action was outlined in secrecy, "as Bose and Hitler would have done." On the day of the oil distribution, Master Goyal's class would refuse to disperse after the morning assembly, and start chanting the slogan *"le ke rahin ge: tel ke pipe"* (we demand; cans of oil). One of us was designated to shout the first part of the slogan, to which all the others would respond with the second part.

The plan was successfully kept secret and duly carried out. Our slogans that morning caused a sensation. The headmaster, bewildered, immediately postponed the oil distribution and ordered our class back to the classroom. Over the next day or two, the news that headmaster and Master Goyal were on a collision course spread through the school and even into the bazaar. It split the student community. Rafiq, who was then in the last year of school, took the headmaster's side; I supported Master Goyal. I well remember the tension in the school: young Master Goyal versus the aging Headmaster Bhalla, dynamic Bose versus fawning Gandhi. Finally, a group of 'prominent citizens' from the town went to see the headmaster, who gave in and allowed the students to control the oil distribution. For Master Goyal, though, it was a Pyrrhic victory, as he was soon transferred to another school. We never saw him again.

In the 1990s, when I visited India for the first time after Independence, I was surprised to see Bose's portrait everywhere. His round, pudgy face, with Coke-bottle spectacles, was hanging alongside Gandhi's on the walls of *dhabas*, newsstands and *pan* shops. Why revere a man who wanted to be the Hitler of India? In Pakistan and Britain, Bose is hardly ever mentioned. A retired professor in the waiting room of the Varanasi railway station tried to explain Bose's popularity to me. "We Indians have to overcome our historic inferiority complex. For centuries, we were overrun by a small number of invaders, first the Muslims, and then the British. We did not have the unity, will and determination to stop them. So, in a way, Bose, though he was unsuccessful in his immediate objective, showed us the way. Gandhian tactics could not have stopped the Muslim or the British."

3

"What do you think of Jinnah's two-nation theory?" asked Ramzan Ali. The question was not directed at any one person in particular. It was early 1946, and Ramzan Ali, Ravi Saroop, Bansi Lal, Dr. Muhammad Husain, Joginder Singh, and my father were sitting under one of the mango trees.

There were two big mango trees besides our house, one on the east side and one on the south. The shade of the one on the south was used for socializing; the one on the east had our water buffalo tied under it. Our house was right behind the hospital. Every evening, one of the servants put a few chairs in a circle under the tree. In the summer months, the *bahishti* sprinkled water on the ground from his *mashk* before putting the chairs. The water eased the heat and settled the dust.

"I don't know what a nation is," said Ravi. "Is it not just people with different set of customs? If so, then we have many nations, not just two. In Mukerian here we not only have Muslims and Hindus but also Sikhs, Christians, and *Chamars*."

"Ravi has a point," my father said. He generally sided with Ravi but more than anything else always tried to find the middle ground.

"I know what Ravi is saying;" said Ramzan. "But Hindus and Muslims are the two dominant groups. They say that two beggars can sleep on one bed, but two kings cannot share a kingdom. Same with the Muslims and the Hindus." We had heard this 'beggars and kings' analogy from Ramzan before.

"Jinnah should know that as for as Punjab is concerned, there are three nations, Hindus, Muslims and Sikhs," Joginder said.

There were a total of about ten people in my father's circle of friends, of which at least three or four usually dropped by every evening. My father was not always there, for he could be occupied with an emergency at the hospital, but this did not matter as the others carried on the conversation. Ramzan was usually accompanied by his *hookahbardar* who carried Ramzan's *hookah* and periodically freshened the *chillum* with tobacco, which the *hookahbardar* carried in a pouch. Rafiq and I were allowed to sit among the adults, though we never joined the conversation nor were we expected to do so. Only occasionally, someone, out of boredom, asked us about our school or homework. Needless to say, there were never any women.

Of all these friends, Ramzan and Joginder were the most impressive-looking. Ramzan was very tall and well built, with a large hooked nose. He had a moustache and a beard, both nicely trimmed. It was his *pugree* which set him apart. Made of starched white linen, it was wrapped around a *kulla* and had a prominent *turra* which stood straight up. The *pugree* made him look even taller and more impressive. He was always dressed in neat white freshly laundered *shalwar-kamiz*. No one could mistake him for someone other than a refined Muslim. He was an *arthi* who bought produce, like cotton and wheat, from the farmers and sold it to retailers. Sometimes he sold the produce directly to the government. He also owned substantial land in a nearby village. In the agricultural society of India, land was the preeminent sign of wealth. Land was what you invested your money in, if you had any. There was no bank in Mukerian, though it was possible to keep a passbook account in the local post office, but few did.

Joginder Singh, as you can guess from his name, was a Sikh. Like Ramzan, he was tall and, with a Sikh turban and full-sized *kirpan*, he cut a dashing figure. He was a prominent landholder and was very influential in the Sikh community. He had a loud voice and was rather imperious but was always nice to my father. Joginder's large family frequently required my father's medical services. My father often went to his house on the bicycle, with his black medical bag tied to the carrier on the back, to see one or another of the ailing members of Joginder's extended family.

Muhammad Husain was the local veterinary surgeon, popularly called a *dungar* doctor. He wore a red *roomi topi*, which was the local name for a fez. Made of felt, the *roomi topi*, with its prominent tassel, must have come to India from Turkey and was worn only by Muslims. I remember that Dr. Husain's servant occasionally brought fresh meat in the morning to our house. You see, Dr. Husain, as the *dungar* doctor, had to certify all the animals which were butchered daily in Mukerian by the *kesais*. So the *kesais* took turns in sending some free meat to the *dungar* doctor as a gift, which Dr. Husain was happy to share with our family. One of Dr. Husain's sons attended A.S.High School but was not in my class.

Of the Hindu friends, Bansi Lal was the most regular attendant, though he rarely participated in the conversation. Being our neighbour, he did not have to come far. Bansi Lal was of medium height but thin and reedy. He wore a shirt and *dhoti* and a circular cloth cap. He was soft-spoken and very kind. He was a Brahmin and was therefore often addressed as Panditji. His son Amrit was a year or two older than I and played with both me and Rafiq. Mrs. Bansi Lal often cooked delightful sweetmeats, like *gulab jamins*, which she sent to our house. As Bansi Lal's family was Brahmin, non-Hindus were not allowed to enter their house. I remember one evening while we were playing football (soccer), the ball went inside Bansi Lal's house through the open front door. Instinctively, I ran into the house to retrieve the ball. Amrit's mother was in a panic and asked me to leave the house immediately. She then washed the floor where I had stepped. It may seem strange now, but this was all part of their religion, and nobody seemed to be upset by it.

Ravi Saroop was a Hindu cloth merchant. Like Ramzan, he appeared to be a man of wealth. He was a voluble man who had strong opinions. Unlike the others, Ravi had been active in politics for a long time. He was a long-standing supporter of the Congress Party. Ravi was unequivocally committed to a united free India.

"I personally don't like the two-nation theory either," said Ramzan. "But the point is, if the British leave, can we keep India in one piece? I believe that as soon as the British leave there is going to be fighting all over India, like it was before the British. Is it not better to stay under the British rule as one country?" Ramzan's family had obviously done well under the British and he was suspicious of both the Congress Party and the Muslim League.

"Well, most Indians want independence. We don't want to live under *angrezi raj* forever, do we?" said Ravi Saroop.

"What is wrong with *angrezi raj*?" Ramzan asked.

"Well, what is good about it?" was Ravi's rejoinder.

"I tell you, *angrezi raj* has been good for us," said Ramzan. "My grandmother could remember the times before the British when there was no law and order." As Joginder was present this evening, Ramzan did not elaborate on the pre-English times of his grandmother. What Ramzan was referring to was the *Sikhon ka zamana*, the Sikh era, under Maharaja Ranjit Singh. Ramzan had a great collection of Sikh stories in which Sikhs were portrayed as ignorant, bumbling people, and Ranjit Singh as their strong but arbitrary ruler. "You know how Ranjit Singh was?" went one of Ramzan's stories. "Ranjit believed in equal justice for all. One day he had to pass judgment on twenty criminals. He had drunk too much *bhang* and was in a hurry. So he divided the criminals into two groups of ten each and ordered one group to be hanged and the other to be set free. Equal justice, you see." In one set of Sikh jokes, called *bara baje* jokes, the so-called 'midday jokes', the incidents always took place at midday when, because of the heat and their long hair, the Sikhs supposedly went a little crazy. As I said, Ramzan told these jokes when Joginder was not around, though the jokes were told in good humour and without malice. No doubt, the Sikhs had plenty of Muslim jokes. They were like the Irish or Ukrainian jokes.

"And how about all the roads, dams, hospitals and railways that the British have built?" Ramzan continued.

"Look, Ramzan," said Ravi, "we had roads long before the British had them in their own country. Sher Shah Suri built the *Jarnaili Sarak*[1] many hundred years before *angrez* set foot in India.

We had magnificent buildings. We would have done much better without them. They destroyed our civilization in 1857."

4

The Indian Mutiny of 1857 was a subject of which our friends talked endlessly. The story in our history book gave the standard British account of the mutiny, but the teachers were beginning to give an Indian spin to the events. We talked about the mutiny at home, too. Many of the characters, especially on the Indian side, were household names: Bahadur Shah Zafar, Rani of Jhansi, Nana Fernavis, Tantia Topi. My father had an Urdu translation of a book about the mutiny written by a British woman who lived through it. The writer's husband, an army officer, was brutally killed by the *sepoys* but the woman and her two children were rushed by a faithful Indian servant through the back door and hidden in a sugarcane field till help arrived. In addition to her poignant personal experiences, the writer delved considerably into the causes of the mutiny.

Between what I read in the school books, what my teachers were telling, what the friends under the tree said in the evenings, and what the British woman had written, I was confused. What actually happened in 1857?

The two native players in the mutiny were the *sepoys* in the service of the East India Company, and the native rulers. India was a vast rumour-mill where rumours travelled from village to village at amazing speed. Indians saw sinister motives behind every move made by those in power, and they had ample historical reasons to do so. The *sepoys* believed the rumours that the British were determined to convert them to Christianity. On their part, the native rulers were smarting from the loss of their power. Unfortunately, both of these grievances, imagined and real, coincided.

Religious grievances, whether those of *sepoys* or of civilians, were a mixed bag. The British had taken some measures which were contrary to orthodox Hindu beliefs. In 1832 British outlawed *suttee* and made determined efforts to stamp out female infanticide. *Suttee* was the age-old Hindu custom of the voluntary self-immolation of a wife on her dead husband's burning funeral pyre. Such immolations could be far from voluntary, however. Newly-made widows were often goaded by relatives anxious to get their hands on the dead man's possessions. Female infanticide was practiced to avoid the horrendous dowry costs which Hindu fathers had to pay to marry off their daughters. In addition, in 1856 the government passed legislation allowing Hindu widows to remarry. For centuries Hindu widows were the very emblem of tragedy; unable to remarry, they were outcasts in their own family. It is true that many educated Hindus were not particularly upset by these British measures, as they themselves felt such beliefs and customs were antiquated, if not repugnant. But the well-intentioned and cautiously liberal British legislation sparked the rumours that these were the first steps towards converting Indians to Christianity.

However, the East India Company was a European trading company, and though its power over time had increased enormously, its driving force was trade, not religion. Like any other trading company, its board of directors' primary responsibility was to make profit for its shareholders. True, in the wake of the East India Company, a few missionaries had come to India, but they did nothing more than convert a few Untouchables to Christianity (and no doubt the Untouchables were grateful for the little self-respect they gained from this conversion). The fact that the Christians currently comprise only 2.3 percent of the Indian population shows that no organized effort was made to convert people. Though the reforms were primarily directed at Hindu customs, Muslims too looked upon the East India Company as an infidel ruler which had successfully supplanted centuries of Muslim power. Muslim sentiment was no doubt exploited by the *mullahs* with their cry of 'Islam is in danger'. Not surprisingly, many Muslim fighters died shouting *"Din, Din"* (religion, religion).

The native rulers' loss of power was slow but inexorable. Even a cursory study of the rise of the East India Company's power and the corresponding decline of native power shows how unwittingly the Company gained its dominance. Repeatedly, the company directors in London wanted to call a halt to its expansion, but the Company was often forced into conflicts because of the infighting among the native rulers. Often these rulers, knowing the superior fighting power of the company, intentionally dragged it into their internecine conflicts

In 1857 Bahadur Shah Zafar was only a nominal emperor whose writ did not extend beyond the Red Fort in Delhi. He was 82 and living on a generous British pension, writing poems (he was a good Urdu poet). Without British protection he would have lost his throne, if not his head, long before. There is good evidence that Zafar was not in favour of the rebellion and that his hand was forced by the mutinous rag-tag *sepoys* who suddenly stormed the fort, declaring him emperor of all India, and asking him to lead them against the British. He had to make an instant decision whether to accept the offer or be forever branded a spineless traitor.

Rani of Jhansi's case is more complex. She is viewed by many Indians through a veil of tears, and no doubt was the only Indian leader of the mutiny worthy of respect. She was an exceptionally brave woman and had an arguably-justified, though purely personal, cause to fight the British. Rani was upset with the so-called Doctrine of Lapse introduced by Lord Dalhousie. Simply put, the doctrine meant that if the ruler of a state, which had accepted the British paramountcy, died without a legitimate biologic heir, the state would be annexed by the East India Company. The doctrine was contrary to the Hindu tradition, which allowed an adopted child to inherit the throne. No doubt, the Doctrine of Lapse was unfair to the native rulers and was a British way to expand their possessions. This expansionist policy was founded on the belief, especially espoused by Dalhousie, that the Indian people would be better off under British rule with its liberal ideas and strong institutions of public service than under any native ruler. After all, it was Dalhousie who had introduced three of the most stunning advances in India, i.e., the railway, the telegraph, and the postal service. No doubt, many native rulers were more than happy to accept British paramountcy, as it protected them from both outside invasion and internal rebellion, thus giving them free hand to enjoy their wealth. The British, however, failed to comprehend the force of tradition in India, which was, and still is, strong and can thwart any liberal initiative.

The third major player, Nana Sahib, was the adopted son of the last Maratha *peshwa*, Baji Rao. Baji Rao was a venal, corrupt man whose life of intrigue and self-indulgence was legendry. It is enough to say that Baji Rao was lucky to be allowed by the British to retire near Cawnpore on a comfortable pension of one hundred thousand pounds a year with which he continued to live a life of great luxury, though hounded, we are told, by ghosts of those he had killed mercilessly in his early life. Nana Sahib lost the title of *peshwa* after his father's death but still retained Baji's vast fortune. Loss of the prestigious title of *peshwa* angered Nana and he appealed first to Lord Dalhousie and then to the company's board of directors to reverse the decision, but his appeals were rejected. Furious at the rejections, Nana secretly got in touch with various disaffected rulers in India, though outwardly he remained amiable and charming to the British, entertaining them lavishly. When the mutiny broke out, Nana saw his chance but, before committing himself, he wanted to make sure that he was on the winning side. Nana first offered to help his British friends in Cawnpore but later, seeing the early reverses suffered by the British, he deceived the British and joined the rebels. It was Nana who allowed, if not personally ordered, the merciless butchery of British women and children in Cawnpore, an event which was to become the rallying cry for British retribution.

It was therefore obvious that all the notable Indian figures in the mutiny had personal motives and none of them had any intention of forming a united independent India.

Whenever anyone talked of the 1857 Mutiny, the term 'greased cartridges' was immediately mentioned. They were new cartridges which had to be bitten by mouth before being loaded with a ramrod into the muzzle of the Enfield rifle. The rumour spread that the grease contained a mixture of cow and pig fat, thus defiling both Hindus and Muslims in one convenient 'bite'. The grease was actually a mixture of linseed oil and beeswax, but no amount of explanation, or even the withdrawal of the cartridges, was enough to appease the *sepoys*. The rumour of the greased cartridges, though the most widely quoted, was not the only rumour then circulating. It was also said that the flour used to make *chapatis* for the *sepoys* contained ground-up animal bones. Passing rumours along, with progressive embellishment, was the favourite social pastime of the Indian villagers on long summer afternoons.

Ravi always called the Mutiny of 1857 *Jang-e-azadi*. "It was our greatest tragedy that we lost that war in 1857," he said with evident sorrow.

"And why did we lose the war?" Ramzan asked.

"Because we were not united," replied Ravi. "Some of the *nawabs* and rajas became traitors and took the English side."

"And after the *angrez* won, they quartered their horses in Taj Mahal and *Jama Masjid*," Muhammad Husain chipped in.

"And with due respect to Joginder," Ravi said, looking at Joginder, "the Sikhs did not help."

Joginder had his ready answer. "But look how the Mughal rulers treated the Sikhs. They tried damn hard to exterminate us. They killed Guru Gobindji[2]. Why should have Sikhs helped? The Sikhs knew that if the British were defeated, the Mughals would persecute the Sikhs again."

"This is exactly the point I am making," said Ramzan. "If the mutiny had succeeded, it would have been followed by a terrible conflict between Indians."

"Okay, forget 1857," Ravi said with some exasperation. "Now is the time for unity. We can now work together and keep India united."

"Believe me, if the British leave there will be chaos. *Goondas* will rule the country," Ramzan insisted.

"*Goondas* are controlled by the police, and the government controls the police," replied Ravi. "Once we have our own government, we will have no *goondas*."

True, the police did not have good reputation. One day my father heard that *dacoits* had broken into the house of one of his friends in a nearby village and, brandishing swords, had ransacked the house. My father, Rafiq, and I went on a *tonga* to our friend's house. There were two or three policemen there, along with the *thanidar*. The *thanidar* and the policemen were sitting under the tree outside the house and were enjoying a delicious dinner of chicken curry. Our friend took my father aside and said to him tearfully, "I have been providing board and lodging to the policemen for the last three days. The *thanidar* demands eggs for breakfast and a *murghi* for dinner every day. In the meantime the only thing they have done is to take my statement."

Dr. Husain generally supported Ravi as far as the Indian independence was concerned, but secretly he nursed a different reason for it. Dr. Husain was convinced that once the British left, Muslims would take control of India. Like some other Muslims, he followed the simple logic that if Muslims had ruled India for 700 years before the British arrival, they could do so again once the British left. Later on, when it became obvious to Muslims like Dr. Husain that a free India would be perpetually ruled by its Hindu majority, they naturally aligned themselves with Jinnah, who was increasingly talking of a separate homeland for the Muslims.

5

It was at about this time that I remember making my first visit to Mirpur, our ancestral village. Mirpur was about two miles from Dasuya, which was a railway station on the line from Mukerian to Jalandhar. From Dasuya we walked on a dirt path to Mirpur, though occasionally my father sent a messenger in advance, telling the relatives in the village the date and time of our train arrival and asking for someone from the village to come and meet us at the station on a *gada*. My mother and my sisters observed *purdah* and put on *burqas* whenever they were out of the house; my mother wore the old-fashioned 'shuttlecock' type, while my sisters wore the more modern two-piece outfit. Interestingly, they did not wear *burqas* in the village and went about quite freely like all the other women in the village. I am not sure why this was so; perhaps in the village people looked upon everyone as part of one large family. My father rarely came with us to Mirpur. It was usually my mother who took us. It was safe for women and children to travel without a male escort in those days, thanks to the *angrezi raj*, as my mother used to say.

Mirpur was a typical Punjabi village, congested, dirty, with no electricity, running water or sanitation. This was hardly surprising, considering that Mukerian, much larger, had none of these services. Mirpur was predominantly a Muslim village, with some Hindu and Sikh families. Individual villages, though by no means segregated, tended to have people of one religion. They lived in impressive harmony, and we never heard of any minority member in a village being harassed in any way[3]. In Mirpur, *kacha* houses were stacked next to each other with open sewers running outside. I have no idea where those sewers discharged their effluent. There was virtually no greenery in the village itself, except for an occasional spindly tree in a courtyard. The source of drinking water was a couple of wells. Fortunately, the water table was high and the water was therefore easily accessible and not brackish as in some other villages. One well had a simple bucket at the end of the rope while the other had a more elaborate buckets-on-wheel system operated by a bull. This second well provided water to a small vegetable garden. The land otherwise was not irrigated, and depended on seasonal rain for cultivation. My *dada*, Ishaq, had left the village as a young man and had joined the Punjab Police. *Dada* left home because *dada's* father died young and *dada* did not get along with his uncle, who had assumed the care of the family. Fortunately, *dada* had attended a school in Dasuya where he had learned to read and write Urdu. On joining the police he was encouraged to learn a little more Urdu, so that he could write police reports which, since the days of the Mughals, were written in Urdu. *Dada* Ishaq did well in the police and became a *thanidar*, which was about as high as he could go. This was quite an achievement for a poor village boy. With the money he saved, he bought land just outside Mirpur and built a house where he eventually retired. It was a *kacha* house with two big rooms, a veranda and a large courtyard. I have only a vague memory of *dada* Ishaq. He was diabetic and died of fever. My father's widowed sister, Auntie Noor, now lived in that house with her only son, Arif.

This visit to Mirpur with my mother was the result of the news, brought by a man from the village, that the *dada's* house had been broken into, and the contents of one room had been stolen. Most of the stolen things belonged to us. These were things like *durries*, blankets, sheets and some utensils, which my mother had stored there because my father was often transferred from place to place. The idea was that we would collect them when my father built his retirement home in Dasuya. It was a summer night when the theft occurred, when Auntie Noor and Arif were sleeping in the courtyard. The thieves entered the house by making a large hole in the back wall of one of the rooms and took everything from that room. Since the house was made of mud, it was not difficult to make the hole and it was a fairly standard method of thievery in those days. It appeared likely that the thieves knew the contents of the rooms, as they broke into the room in which our relatively more expensive belongings were kept. Auntie Noor's room was not entered. There was not much we could do about the theft. Nobody bothered to inform the police. There was no policeman in Mirpur and the nearest *thana* was in Dasuya. In any case, little was expected from the police.

Gandhi for many years had waxed eloquent on the Indian villages, the fresh air, good food, the self-sufficiency of the villagers and so on. In fact, he promoted the boycott of foreign (i.e., British) goods to foster traditional Indian village life. I, on the contrary, found village life hardscrabble and miserable.

Diseases such as gastroenteritis, malaria, and tuberculosis were rife. There were people sitting under the trees coughing their lungs out. As no medicines were available, not even herbal ones, the villagers depended on prayers, charms, and amulets. Whatever their religion, the villagers' beliefs always included a large dose of omens, folklore and superstition. All children, especially the boys who were prized, had amulets around their necks or arms. Among the Muslims the amulets usually contained verses from the Quran.

Food was always scarce, limited to *chapatis*, lentils, and occasional vegetables in season. Mango in season was the only plentiful fruit, though occasionally one saw *ber* and *jaman* for sale. In the morning we went out into the fields to relieve ourselves. As so many other people had the same idea in the morning it was difficult to find a private spot to do the job. There was no paper or water; you simply had to find some leaves to clean up afterwards[4]. It was especially difficult for women as they had to go out in the dark, early in the morning or later at night. Nobody talked about these problems or did anything about them.

One day, while we were staying in Mirpur, news came that a *tiddydul* had landed the previous night in the neighbouring village. The people were agitated and directions went out by word of mouth: "Take drums or empty tin cans and fill them with stones. Scatter yourselves in the fields and stay there till nightfall. If the *tiddydul* approaches your field, make as much noise as you can." Locusts settle down in the evening, and wherever they settle the crops are destroyed within a few hours. The idea was to make enough noise so that the locusts wouldn't settle in your field. If someone had to lose his livelihood, it better be someone in the next village.

Later in the day, the *tiddydul* appeared on the horizon. It was truly an incredible sight. The cloud flew overhead for about fifteen minutes. An occasional locust dropped to the ground but that did not matter because the main cloud kept going. Our village was saved!

There was a seasonal runoff stream near our village. We called it a *cho*. Most of the year it was dry but in rainy season water could suddenly come rushing down in it whenever it rained heavily on the hills. As any unwary passerby crossing the *cho* was likely to be swept away, we were told not to go near the *cho* in monsoon season. Older people said that they remembered an occasional cheetah being washed down the *cho* and becoming a menace to the villagers.

6

I remember going to my mother's village too, for the first and only time. It was called Chak Mehran and it was a mile or so from Mirpur. My *nani* had suddenly passed away. There was not enough time to go to the funeral as burial among Muslims is done within 24 hours of death, so we went to the customary mourning ritual on the fortieth day after death. My maternal grandparents were very poor and lived in a small mud house. They had very little land. My *nana* was a frail old man with a wispy beard. He was also the local Sufi *pir* and had many *murids* in the village who came to him for advice and blessing. They also brought presents like eggs, chickens, and local fruit in season which helped *nana* feed his family.

"How did *nani* die?" I asked

"Your *nani*," he said, "had an ulcer on her chest, the one with roots. There is no treatment for it. The roots got deeper and deeper till they reached every part of her body. She became extremely thin. The ulcer, you see, was sucking all the nourishment. One morning she just did not wake up." My father later told me it was breast cancer.

"And then what did you do?" This was my first experience of death in my family and I was curious.

"We buried her according to our Muslim custom," my *nana* said. "Her body was washed by the female relatives and friends, and then we wrapped her in a single white sheet. We carried her on a *charpoy* to the *kabristan* and buried her with her face turned to Mecca."

"Who carried the *charpoy*? It must be heavy," I asked.

"Four people carried it on their shoulders. It is our custom that most family members and close friends take turns 'giving the shoulder'."

The following day my mother took me to my *nani's* grave. My *nana* and one other relative accompanied us. The *kabristan* was a short walk from the village. It was bleak and dusty with no grass or tree. *Nani's* grave was *kacha*, like all the other graves in that *kabristan*. As I said, it was a poor village and families could not afford brick and mortar to make *pacca* graves. *Kacha* graves rarely lasted long and disappeared in a few years, making room for the fresh ones. We stood beside the grave and the adults raised their hands and prayed to Allah quietly. I did not know any prayer but nonetheless raised my hands. My mother and *nana* were crying but I could not because I hardly knew my *nani*.

On the fortieth day after my *nani's* death, a number of friends and relatives arrived, mostly from Chak Mehran but a few came from surrounding villages. I sat outside on *charpoys* with the men, while women assembled inside in the courtyard. A small amount of uncooked rice was brought out and each of us took a handful. The rice grains were thrown on a piece of cloth which was spread out on the ground in the centre, and one of Allah's ninety-nine names was uttered with each throw of the grain. Afterwards, sweet *chai* was served in small metal tumblers. Curiously, no mention of my *nani* was made; men merely talked of the crops and the seasons.

7

As the Independence appeared inevitable, we began to have invited speakers at the morning assembly in school. This was new, as the morning assembly had always been for prayer and announcements. The political parties were now putting pressure on the headmaster to allow party workers to talk to the students. The British, I suppose, had decided that as they were now going to leave India anyway, what was taught and what was learned in the schools was no longer their concern. One morning the invited speaker was a Muslim. He was neatly dressed in an *achkin* and a *karakul* cap. He was a member of the Congress Party, and no doubt the Party was promoting his tour to show that the Party had both Hindu and Muslim members. He talked of the golden era which awaited a free and united India. "The tyranny of the *angrezi raj* is coming to an end," he said. "They will not be able to shed the blood of innocent Indians anymore. We will not have another Jallianwalla," he thundered as he raised his right arm. The Jallianwalla Bagh massacre was not news to us. Though it happened in 1919, people talked about it as if it was yesterday's event. The Indian leaders and the vernacular press had never ceased to dwell on it. Ravi often mentioned it as yet another example of British brutality.

In 1915, during World War I, the Defense of India Act was passed by the Government of India to ensure wartime security. It allowed the government to arrest and detain, without appeal, anyone who was suspected of sedition or espionage. As wartime measures go, it was neither unique nor unreasonable, as long as it was applied judiciously, which it was. There were no mass arrests, no summary executions.

After the war, the Indians expected some peace dividends. After all, they had contributed substantially to the war effort. Indians volunteered in millions to fight, and the Princely States contributed heavily to the war chest. Britain should have been grateful to them, and she was. It should be noted, however, that the British Indian Army, though a great institution, was a mercenary army. The Indian soldier was not fighting for "King and Country" but for the paycheck with which he supported the family back in the Punjab or Nepal. As for the Princely States, they supported the war effort out of self-interest, as they knew full well that their very existence depended on the survival of the British Raj. In the meantime, the government, still worried about security, though the war had ended, appointed a committee under Justice Sir Sydney Rowlatt to review the security situation. This was the time of Bolshevik

Revolution, and the committee, concerned about a communist-inspired insurgency in India, recommended that the wartime measures be extended for at least another six months. The committee overestimated the threat of communist subversion in India, and the so-called Rowlatt Acts, approved in March 1919, were unnecessary.

Gandhi's supposedly 'non-violent' protest against the Rowlatt Acts now began to spread with inevitable violence throughout India. Gandhi announced that April 6 was to be a day of *hartal* to protest the Rowlatt Acts. *Hartal*, in theory, means a day of voluntary and peaceful closure of businesses and services to protest an unpopular measure. In actual practice *hartal* in India was never totally voluntary or peaceful. Gangs of activists and troublemakers roamed the streets, assaulting and intimidating those who refused to close their shops. The gangs often then moved to government buildings and offices, throwing stones, breaking windows and lighting fires. Confrontation with the police was inevitable.

After announcing his opposition to the Rowlatt Acts and calling for *hartal*, Gandhi announced his decision to come to the Punjab to 'rouse' the masses. Sir Michael O'Dwyer, Lieutenant Governor of Punjab, thought it prudent to stop Gandhi from entering the province. O'Dwyer also arrested two popular local Indian leaders in Amritsar, an important city in the Punjab, who were making violent pro-independence speeches, and ordered them removed from the city. A crowd estimated at many thousands gathered and, thinking that their leaders were being put on a train, moved towards the railway station. Stopped by a Gurkha battalion from reaching the railway station, the crowd then tried to make its way to the deputy commissioner's residence. Here, when some people in the crowd tried to storm the residence, they were met by the police, resulting in a number of casualties.

By evening, a number of buildings in the city, including banks and the city hall, were aflame. Telegraph lines were cut, train service disrupted, and violent and menacing crowds gathered here and there. A number of Europeans were attacked and some killed. An English missionary woman, who had lived in Amritsar for 15 years and happened to be cycling through the bazaar, was severely beaten, causing great resentment in the local British community.

Was it all sliding out of control? Was it 1857 all over again? Gandhi had been arrested but that had made matters worse. It is certain that at least some in the government were gravely concerned

A public gathering was called in the Jallianwalla Bagh, a garden near the Golden Temple in Amritsar, on April 13, though public gatherings of more than five persons were prohibited under the emergency measures. Some Indian writers have described the gathering as an innocent family picnic. Perhaps many who gathered there were innocent, but the organizers were not. Anti-government, pro-independence speeches were planned and delivered. The person in charge of enforcing the law in the area was Brigadier-General Reginald Dyer who commanded a mainly Gurkha force. Dyer and his force entered the Bagh quietly and Dyer gave orders to shoot without warning. The shooting lasted a few minutes and did not finish till all the ammunition was exhausted and over 400 people killed.

Dyer's explanation of what he did was simple: "People were breaking the law and had to be taught a lesson."

Dyer's response to the Indian crowd's breaking the law was inexcusably excessive and caused enormous controversy at the time. He was called to appear before a commission of enquiry in London. Dyer was supported by some, reviled by others. Governor O'Dwyer of the Punjab congratulated him. The House of Lords commended him, while the House of Commons censured him. The daily *Morning Post* of Britain raised over £25,000 for his defense. His admirers gave him a sword inscribed "Saviour of the Punjab." Churchill was appalled and called the shooting "a monstrous event which stood in sinister isolation in the annals of the British Imperial history." Following the commission of enquiry's report, which was highly critical of him, Dyer was demoted[5].

Before we draw the curtain on Jallianwalla, let us follow the story to its denouement. When in 1919 Governor O'Dwyer was living in his palatial residence in Lahore, a poor Sikh boy, Udham Singh, was growing up in a Sikh orphanage in Amritsar. Later, Udam Singh wandered around the world, doing odd jobs under a variety of names, became an ardent Indian patriot, and eventually arrived in England. Governor O'Dwyer, too, retired to England where he devoted his time to writing about India and about his ancestors, the great O'Dwyers of Ireland. On March 13, 1940, under the assumed name of Ram Mohammad Singh Azad, signifying Hindu, Muslim and Sikh identities (*azad* means free), Udham Singh walked up to the 75-year-old O'Dwyer in Caxton Hall in London and shot him dead. "I was planning it since April 13, 1919," Udam said, before he was hanged[6].

8

One day when Ravi once again took up the topic of Indian independence, and how Gandhi had awakened Indians to the idea of independence, Ramzan said, "Ravi, do you know that the idea of Indian independence was actually a British idea?"

"What do you mean that Indian independence was a British idea?" asked Ravi.

"Precisely that. The idea of Indian independence was introduced into India by the British. Before that, Indians never thought of independence as a nation, only independence of one *nawab* or maharaja from another. Do you know that the Congress Party was actually founded by the British?"

Ravi did not know that. Not many Indians knew or cared to know.

"It was Hume who founded the Congress Party. But Hume wanted independence by negotiation, not confrontation," continued Ramzan. "It was people like Tilak who started promoting violence."

Ramzan told us the early history of Indian independence movement. Ramzan was a Unionist[7] and had heard and read about the early pioneers of Indian independence. He was an anglophile. He admired the British without ever having been to England, or even ever meeting an Englishman. Nobody else among our friends seemed to know about those early pioneers. Others only talked of Gandhi, Jinnah and Nehru.

Allan Hume, besides being a great advocate of Indian independence, was a pioneer of Indian ornithology. This was in addition to his primary job as a very busy public administrator. Trained as a physician in England, he was an indefatigable social reformer in India. Hume was a supporter of women's education, reformer of juvenile delinquents, and opponent of barbaric Indian customs like female infanticide. Though his extensive collection of Indian birds was partly destroyed by a landslide at his home in Simla, and his notes on Indian birds sold by his servant as wrapping paper, he left enough information on Indian birds to be considered one of the greatest ornithologists of India.

Hume lived through the Mutiny of 1857 and was critical of the British for not showing enough sensitivity to Indian culture. On many other issues Hume was willing to cross swords with the British. He supported Indian Home Rule and, with Annie Besant, founded the Indian National Congress, commonly called the Congress Party, in 1885, with full approval of Lord Dufferin, then Viceroy of India. The Congress Party led the Indian Independence Movement and has ruled India for most of the time since independence. The fact that the British government itself was considering Home Rule for India as early as the end of the nineteenth century clearly meant that they had no intention of staying in India forever.

Annie Besant was one of those accomplished eccentrics which Britain has regularly produced in its long history. Born in England as Annie Woods in 1847, she married a clergyman, Frank Besant, at an early age but divorced him and rejected Christianity. She became a member of such organizations as the Secular Society and the Fabian Society. She was a popular member of the London School Board, an early advocate of birth control, a brilliant speaker, an inveterate pamphleteer, and a friend of George Bernard Shaw. She encouraged workers in factories to demand better working conditions and became famous in England for organizing the working women in the factory of Bryant and May, manufacturers of matches (an important consumer product in those days). She also took active interest in theosophy[8], a type of philosophy which appears to have some elements of Buddhist and Hindu thinking. She first came to India in 1894 and plunged herself into the promotion of Home Rule for Indians. She had the wholehearted support of both Muslims and Hindus. Annie became the secretary general, and in 1917, president of the Congress Party.

No minority, for its numbers, has done more for India than Parsis. Dadabhai Naoroji was just such a Parsi. Born in 1825 in Gujarat of a poor Parsi family, he worked his way up by sheer determination and hard work. After his schooling in Bombay he went to England where he started his own business, wrote books, and became a professor at the University College in London. On his return to India, Naoroji, with Hume and others, worked for the Congress Party whose president he became in 1886. He went back to England and was elected MP for Finsbury Central (and immediately nicknamed 'Mr. Narrow Majority' for winning his seat with a majority of only three votes). Naoroji, when inducted as an MP, was allowed to swear on his Parsi scriptures, instead of the Bible. In the British parliament he spoke in support of Indian Home Rule (and of Irish Home Rule, too, for that matter). He was a staunch moderate and believed that Indians could attain Home Rule by patient negotiations. Incidentally, the young Indian who supported him in England was the brilliant lawyer, Muhammad Ali Jinnah, the future founder of Pakistan. It was a wonderfully satisfactory relationship, the wise old man and his eager, adoring acolyte. They were not overawed by the British. On the contrary, they understood the British parliamentary system, respected it, and were determined to use it to further the Indian cause. They knew, rightly, that Indian Home Rule was within their grasp. In their innocence, they did not foresee the exploitation of obscurantist forces in India by reactionary Indian leaders.

"I don't see how you can call Gandhiji reactionary," said Ravi indignantly.

"No, I don't, but Tilak was," said Ramzan. "And he became President of the Congress party. Thanks to the benevolence of the British, Tilak won a scholarship to Cambridge University, and how did he show his gratitude? By exhorting Indians to kill the British!"

In post-independent India, Bal Gangadhar Tilak has been included in the pantheon of Indian patriots and many call him the *Lokamanya*, the 'revered one'. Tilak was bright but unsavoury; an ultraconservative Hindu who opposed education for women, arguing that it would make them disobedient to their husbands. When the British government cautiously raised the age of consent for marriage from 10 to 12, after many doctors described young girls bleeding to death from sexual trauma, Tilak was indignant. Tilak was against vaccination too and bitterly opposed measures to stamp out an epidemic of plague.

I often think of those evening soirees, with their seemingly-endless conversations between Ramzan, Ravi, Bansi Lal, Muhammmad Husain, Joginder and others, talking and laughing. They all had different opinions but they were good friends. There was a camaraderie which, to my young mind, was destined to last forever. And yet it all ended suddenly, as if demolished by a cataclysmic earthquake. Were we living in a dream ?

9

How can I write of those years leading up to 1947, without talking about Dhari Ram? In the cobweb of my memories he holds a special place. Dhari Ram was one of the servants employed at the hospital. He had taken the job just before my father was transferred to Mukerian. Dhari was very tall, well over six feet, and very good looking. His sinuous limbs and chiseled features gave him an appearance of great beauty. It was as if he wanted to say to the world, "Look at me. I may only be a lowly servant, born into a low caste, but nature has taken greater pride in making me than in you, Brahmins and all." Dhari was very dark, as Hindus of lower caste often are.

Dhari lived alone in the small one-room house in the hospital compound. In his spare time he did pushups. He kept a big stone in front of his house which he lifted to exercise his arms. He told us that there were not many people strong enough to lift that stone. Rafiq, Amrit and I were his acolytes, though I, being the youngest and having less homework, spent more time with him. Dhari was very fond of me. One day, soon after we arrived in Mukerian, Dhari asked my father if he could learn to cycle. My father let him use his bicycle and Dhari soon became a reasonable, though never a very confident, cyclist. I don't think it is easy to become a confident cyclist unless you have learned to cycle in your childhood. In the evenings, after the day's work, Dhari often took me for a bicycle ride, with me sitting on the carrier at the back. We usually cycled along the dirt road which led to the Beas River. On the way we rested at an old abandoned *haveli*. The *haveli* was very old, made of small red bricks, and only parts of its walls had survived. In the middle of the *haveli* was an abandoned well with its broken parapet made of the same red bricks. We sat down on the parapet of the well.

"Dhari, how old is this place?" I asked.

"I don't know, but it is very old. Perhaps it was built in the Sikh era, or even back in the Muslim period."

"Do we know who lived here?"

"I don't. Perhaps it was built by a rich man as a hunting lodge. You see, in those days there was a lot of game here, tigers, antelopes."

"Why did the rich owner abandon it?"

"Could be any reason. He might have lost favour with the ruler. He and his family might have died in an epidemic. My grandfather used to tell us of a terrible epidemic of plague when the whole villages were emptied of living people. Most of my grandfather's family died, too."

"Where did the plague come from?" I asked.

"Only *paramatma* knows," Dhari said looking towards the sky.

Sitting there on the broken parapet of the well, with bats suddenly shooting out of the crevices of the tumbling walls in the waning light, I imagined a giant dark monster, called plague, walking from village to village, leaving only dead behind.

"It is time to go home," Dhari said, as the jackals began their nightly howls.

Dhari had an incredible repertoire of stories. He could tell a different story every day. He told us these stories in the evenings on summer nights when it was cool and pleasant to be outside under the tree. The mosquitoes were a problem but we had a large supply of oil of citronella, though Dhari never used it. Three of us, Rafiq, Amrit, and I, lay on the *charpoys* while Dhari squatted on the ground with his *hookah*. I think he mixed *bhang* with his tobacco. *Bhang* grew wild in that area.

The stories Dhari told us were often about old royal families. Though some of them were pure fiction, many were based on historical events, about which we had read in school and which had passed into common folklore. It was amazing that Dhari should have heard so many of them. Where had he heard them all, we wondered? He certainly could not have read them for he could not read. Perhaps there was a strong tradition of oral storytelling which, with the introduction of books, was disappearing.

Dhari told us of the Babur's last days. Babur was the first Mughal ruler of India. One day his son, Humayon, became ill. In spite of all the treatment by distinguished *hakims* Humayon's condition worsened. In despair, Babur walked seven times around Humayon's bed and prayed that the illness of Humayon be transferred to his father. Soon Humayon was on his way to recovery, as Babur fell mortally ill.

And he told us of Akbar, the Great Mughal. "Akbar had nine trusted assistants. They were all very clever and were called *navaratna*, which means nine jewels. One of the most trusted was Raja Birbul who was the *wazir-e-azam*. Birbul had a great sense of humour and his repartees, even when made at the expense of the Emperor himself, were a source of great delight to Akbar. One day, Akbar and Birbul, while camping in the countryside, were eating their dinner. Birbul was eating mangoes which Akbar did not like. A camp mule passed by and Birbul offered the mule a mango. The mule sniffed and went on its way. 'You see Birbul, even the mules don't like mangoes,' said Akbar. 'Yes, your majesty, mules don't like mangoes,' replied Birbul." Akbar laughed.

Sometimes, in the evenings, one of us would say, "Dhari, can you tell us another Akbar and Birbul joke?" And Dhari would come up with yet another story.

Many of Dhari's stories were about the princes who had lost their thrones after the death of their fathers and were banished from the land. The struggle for the throne is a constant theme in Indian history. There was never an accepted method of inheritance in India like primogeniture in the West. The death of the father almost always led to a struggle for power among the sons. The wars of succession during the Mughal period, for example, were known to us all. For the aspirant to the throne, it was often *takht ya takhta*.

It was the destruction of Mughal throne by the British in 1857 that provided Dhari with his most poignant stories. The fall of the House of Timur[9] and the forced exile of the last Mughal ruler, Bahadur Shah Zaffar, was a monumental shock to the people of Northern India. An era came to an end in 1857, and what an era it had been! The great Akbar, the imperious Jahangir, the magnificent Shahjehan. It was as if a light had gone out of Indian life in 1857. As long as there was a Mughal emperor, howsoever limited his powers, there was always hope. With the fall of Mughal throne, a curtain came down. The stories that Dhari told us were not so much of Bahadur Shah himself but of his descendents. How the princes and princesses, brought up in the unmatched luxury of the Red Fort, were thrown out, penniless, into the streets! A prince, whose smile could grant a man riches and whose scowl send him to the gallows, was now reduced to begging for food. Dhari knew some of Bahadur Shah's poems, so full of longing and pathos. After all, what was poetry without pathos?

"*Angrez* killed his sons in front of his subjects and exiled the Emperor to Burma," Dhari said of Bahadur Shah.

And whatever the story, Dhari always ended it with the same Punjabi couplets of lamentation.

Not forever nightingale sings in the garden.
Not forever the fun and the frolic.
Not forever our parents, youth and beauty.
Not forever the company of friends.

As he sang, Dhari's voice would break. Whether he was overcome with emotion, or whether it was part of the act, we never knew.

10

Ravi Saroop had yet another bone to pick with the British. It was the belief, then becoming increasingly popular in the Indian middle class and taken up by our history teachers, that the British perpetuated their power in India by deliberately following a policy of 'divide and rule'. In other words, the British played Muslims and Hindus against each other.

Ramzan denounced this allegation. "Britain," he said, "has a democratic parliamentary system, with different parties frequently replacing each other. How can a serious policy of 'divide and rule' be followed by all the parties without it becoming a public knowledge?" After 1857, all major issues pertaining to India were discussed in the Parliament, and questions could be raised by its members. In fact, there were two Indian members of Parliament, Lord Sinha in the House of Lords, and Dadabhai Naoroji in the House of Commons. As far as we know, they never accused Britain of following any kind of divide-and-rule policy. Many prominent Indians became close friends of British politicians, especially in the Labour Party. "Surely, they would have come to know of any such policy," said Ramzan, "if it existed." Many diligent researchers have written books on British India but nobody has ever uncovered any official document supporting a divide-and-rule policy.

"But the British have tried to divide the Indians by promising separate seats to the Muslims," Ravi said. "We are all Indians. Why separate seats for the Muslims?" Ravi had a point. Though Ravi was a conservative Hindu, who believed in Hindu gods, went to his Hindu temple, observed Hindu customs, and was a vegetarian, he sincerely believed that Hindus, Muslims and Sikhs could follow their own religions and yet be part of one India. But were other Indians ready for this? Many Muslims obviously were not, believing that, in the British parliamentary system with 'first past the post', Muslims would always be at the mercy of the Hindus. Muslims themselves had discriminated against Hindus during their rule. Why would Hindus not do the same to Muslims after independence? The Muslims had lobbied the British and the British, sensitive to the Muslim concerns, had promised to give special rights to the Muslims in any future independent India[10]. Ravi maintained that the British assurances to Muslims sowed the seeds of discord between Hindus and Muslims and encouraged Muslims to go their separate way and form their own party, the Muslim League.

To Muslims, British assurances were perfectly reasonable. Rather, or so the Muslims believed, it was unreasonable for the Congress leaders to pretend that Muslims did not exist and that India was populated not by Hindus, Muslims, and Sikhs but by 'Indians'. The Muslim League did not believe that the Indians were ready for such 'enlightened' view, and that it was grossly unrealistic for the Congress, therefore, to look upon British assurances to Muslims as a backward step.

Ironically, both Ramzan and Ravi had the same objective: the emergence of a single, independent, multi-religious India, except that Ramzan wanted to wait for another twenty or thirty years if not indefinitely, while Ravi wanted it right away.

11

My parents wore their religion lightly. In another place, at another time, my father might have called himself a humanist, an agnostic, or even an atheist. But it was different then. Religion was like the clothes you wore. How could you go naked? As I said, I never learned the Quran, or even to say my prayers properly. The only time I was reminded of our religion was twice a year, on *Eid-u-Fitr* and the *Eid-u-Zuha*. *Eid-u Zuha* was a serious occasion, so *Eid-u-Fitr* was the only festive day in the whole year for our family. We did not celebrate birthdays or wedding anniversaries. Few people knew their birthdays anyway, as births were never registered. We called *Eid-u-Fitr,* the *Choti Eid* (the Small Eid) and *Eid-u-Zuha,* the *Bari Eid* (the Big Eid).

Eid-u-Fitr or the *Choti Eid* celebrated the end of the fasting month of Ramadan. I remember my first *Choti Eid* because it caused confusion in the town's Muslim community. Muslims follow a type of lunar calendar, and the first day of the month is determined by the sighting of the moon, which is a very thin crescent to begin with and may not therefore be easily visible in poor weather. The sightings were confirmed by the *mullah*s who received reports from witnesses. It so happened that this time in Mukerian the *mullah*s in the two mosques received conflicting observations; one *mullah* announced the sighting of the moon, the other disagreed. So, two contradictory declarations were made. Most people, including our family, celebrated *Eid* on the first recommended day; people were hungry after a month of fasting and were eager to end the month as soon as possible.

In our family only my sister Hamida fasted in Ramadan. Though I occasionally woke up with her early in the morning to start the fast by eating and drinking, my fast never lasted the whole day. It was no joke fasting in summer when the outside temperature could climb into the high 40s C.

My mother cooked special dishes for *Choti Eid*. One was *sivayyan*, a dish of fine vermicelli noodles; the other was sweet rice with raisins and almonds. She made *sivayyan* a few days before *Eid* out of refined flour which was kneaded and then put through a crude hand-operated noodle-making machine which was fastened to a bed rail. The thread-like vermicelli was then spread on another *charpoy* to be dried in the sun and stored for future cooking.

On the morning of *Choti Eid* we received new clothes and new shoes. Shoes were a mixed blessing as they were made by the local *mochi* out of poorly cured leather, with the result that the leather was very hard and cut through our skin. We rubbed oil into the shoe leather every morning for the first few days to soften the leather. Most of the *Choti Eid* day was spent cooking and eating. My mother made sure food was sent to all neighbours, irrespective of their religion, just as the neighbours shared their food with us on their special days. Nurse Daniel was the only Christian we knew and she never failed to bring some nice food to us on Christmas day. Meat of course could not be shared with Hindus and Sikhs. Hindus were vegetarians and Sikhs did not eat *hilal* meat.

I don't know why the *Bari Eid* was so called. Perhaps it was the notion of sacrifice which took this *Eid* to a higher level. *Bari Eid* was a somber day, when Muslims, who could afford it, sacrificed an animal, the meat of which was partly donated to the poor. My father bought a goat or a sheep a few weeks before *Eid*. On the morning of the *Eid* the local butcher came with hook, rope and knives. The animal was slaughtered in the Muslim *hilal* fashion, then hung from a tree branch outside our house and skinned and chopped. We boys gathered around to see the spectacle. Once, the butcher asked me if I wanted to hold his hand, with the knife in it, when he cut the goat's throat. "You will be rewarded in heaven," he said. My father, who was standing nearby, discreetly stopped me from doing it. The sacrifice is meant to commemorate Allah's command to

Ibrahim (Abraham) to sacrifice his son Ismael. Allah wanted to test if Ibrahim's love for his God was stronger than his love for his son. As Ibrahim prepared to cut Ismael's throat, Allah, satisfied with Ibrahim's loyalty, sent a sheep instead. I had heard that some families encouraged their children to become fond of the sacrificial animal and then made them participate in its slaughter to keep faith with the Abrahamic tradition.

Dr. Husain always invited his Muslim friends, including my father, to the *Eid* prayers in the mosque, after which they all went to Dr. Husain's house for a meal. My father never refused the invitation outright but always made an excuse at the last minute not to go to the mosque but to meet at Dr. Husain's house after the prayers. The excuse was invariably the dreaded attack of gout from which he had suffered all his life. It was a standing joke in the family. A few days before *Eid* my mother would say to us, "I guess it is time your father developed an attack of gout." Almost invariably he would start limping a day or so before *Eid*, claiming that he could not bend to say his prayers. The attack would subside soon after *Eid*. To this day I don't know why he didn't want to go to the mosque. I don't think it was out of any principle, for he was a pragmatic person who was rarely governed by principles, especially those related to religion. He could easily have gone to the mosque to please his Muslim friends. I think it was just that he felt uncomfortable in a house of worship.

Pandit Bansi Lal, besides his son Amrit, had a daughter, Rajini, who was a year or two younger than I and we were quite fond of each other. She would often ask her parents to take me with them when they were going on an outing. Once they took me to see the spectacle of *Ram Lila* which was an annual Hindu drama enacted on the day of *Dussehra*. *Ram Lila* celebrated the defeat of the demon-king, Ravan, by God Ram. In Mukerian it was held outdoors in a large open space. The drama had a spectacular finale with the effigy of Ravan bursting into flames. We all cheered like mad to see Ravan getting his just desserts. The other festival was *Diwali*, celebrating the return of God Ram and his consort Sita from exile. Rafiq and I helped Amrit and Rajini fill small *diwas* with mustard oil and put a wick in each cup. After lighting the wick we carefully put these *diwas* on the wall surrounding the courtyard of their house. Afterwards, Bansi Lal took us for a walk around the town to see the all the *diwas* lit on the Hindu houses and shops. Yet another Hindu festival was *Holi* when people sprinkled coloured water and powder on each other. Generally, my father, being a doctor and a Muslim, was spared the 'fun' of being doused in coloured water, but Amrit made sure that Rafiq and I got our share.

Perhaps the most enjoyable of all the festivals was the *Basant*. *Basant* did not seem to have any religious affiliation, as all the young people participated in it. It was held early in the year when winter was losing its grip. Its dominant theme was the colour yellow and its dominant activity was *patang* flying. People dressed in yellow clothes and flew yellow and other brightly colored *patangs*. We generally made our own *patangs* as they were expensive to buy and you could lose a lot of them, especially if you were a poor *patang* flyer. The crucial component was the string which we treated with gum mixed with crushed glass to make it abrasive. The more abrasive your string, the better your chance of cutting the opponent's string in flight. *Patang* flying was best done standing on high ground which provided better wind. As there was no hill of any kind around, people flew *patangs* from the rooftops. This was dangerous as most houses had no railing around the roof. In the excitement, many people fell off their roofs and ended in the hospital with broken bones. Rafiq and I had a stern order from our father not to fly *patangs* from any rooftop.

12

As the British withdrawal from Indian looked increasing certain, conversation among our friends now took a different turn. "I believe that if British leave India we should form an independent Punjab. Punjab can be a power on its own," Joginder Singh said one evening.

"I agree with that" said Ramzan. "But we don't have Sikander Hayat anymore. If only he were still alive, he would have negotiated with the British for an independent Punjab."

Ramzan and Joginder were convinced that, once the British left, Punjab could be an independent country. It was big and prosperous. Its young men were the sinews of the great Indian Army, whose Sikh and Muslim regiments had legendry reputations. Ramzan, being a Unionist, had been opposed to Gandhi's 'Quit India' movement. Under Sir Sikander Hayat, the Unionist Party's great leader, the party had succeeded in the difficult task of forging an alliance of Hindus, Muslims and Sikhs. On Sir Sikander's death in 1942, his nephew Sir Khizar had come to power but Sir Khizar was less successful. The Muslim League and Congress incessantly ridiculed the Unionist Party and nicknamed it the "Toady Party," for toadying to the British. The name stuck and became so common that many ordinary people seriously called it the Toady Party without knowing what the term meant. Sir Khizar himself was nicknamed *tattoo*, for being the pack animal of the British, and people carried processions through the bazaar chanting *"Toady Party murdabad"* and *"Khizry tattoo hai hai."* Gandhi's incessant needling of the British for immediate and complete independence and Jinnah's emotional call for a separate Muslim haven had successfully emasculated the once-mighty Unionist Party.

13

"Ramzan, you are always saying that we don't need independence. Don't you want to be liberated from the English oppression?" asked Ravi one day.

"I don't see any oppression," replied Ramzan. "Before *angrezi raj* you could not even travel safely. Thugs[11] were everywhere. My grandmother knew of a family who, when travelling, was befriended and then killed by thugs. Their bodies were never found."

I had heard my mother talking of thugs, too. "People were very afraid to travel long distances," she said. "They could never trust anyone when travelling. Thugs posed as normal friendly fellow-travellers and then, finding a suitable opportunity, killed the innocent travellers. I heard of a family who went to *doab* for a wedding and disappeared en route. It was assumed that thugs got them." The very words 'thug' and 'thugee' had passed into our everyday language.

"Still, I don't want to be ruled by the British," Ravi insisted.

"Ravi, let me ask you one question. You talk about freedom from the British. Have you ever met an Englishman?" asked Ramzan.

Ravi had to admit that he had never seen a white man, let alone a bona fide Englishman. "I don't have to meet an Englishman to form my opinion. I can see what they did to India," Ravi said.

Ravi had a very romantic notion of ancient Hindu India. "In Hindu times," Ravi said, "India was known throughout the world as *sone ki chiria*. In Akbar's times too, we were the richest country in the world. Look where we are now under the English."

"What do you think of English people, Doctor Sahib?" Ramzan asked, looking at my father. Those sitting there knew that my father was the only one among that group who had not only seen but had personally known and worked with the English people.

"When I joined the Punjab Medical Service there were many senior English doctors with whom I worked," said my father. "I always found them very fair." As always he said as little as possible. He never liked entering into any discussion.

I knew my parents were thankful for the law and order which the British had established, and for the education and medical care which was now available. After all, my father owed his career in modern medicine to the British and, except for my eldest sister who had stayed home to help my mother, he was successfully sending his children to schools and universities established by the British. True, British had formed a class of their own, though I never heard my father question the racial barriers which the British had discreetly erected. He, himself, though a competent and hard-working doctor, could never have been accepted in the Indian Medical Service (he was in the Punjab Medical Service) which, as the Indian Civil Service, was, at least in the early years, closed to the Indians. My father admired the British without holding any grudge against them. I never heard him railing against the British imperialism, and we were too much in awe of him to ask him about such things. From his occasional comments we knew that he did not like either Gandhi or Jinnah. He thought Gandhi was pushing the buttons of Indian independence too fast. As for Jinnah, he thought Jinnah was driven by personal vanity and felt humiliated because Gandhi, with Nehru's help, had pushed him out of the top echelons of the Congress Party. I had heard him once saying, "I see nothing but disaster in all this bickering between Hindu and Muslim leaders. They should all be sent to *kala pani*."

My father rarely said anything about his early life but I heard much from my mother. "Your father and I were married before your father finished his medical degree in Lahore," she said. "Your father's first posting was to the District Hospital in Multan. It was summer and very hot. You know how Multan is?" And here my mother quoted the well-known Persian couplet popular among the invading conquerors from the North: "Multan offers the visitor four gifts: dust, heat, beggars and graveyards."

"A serious epidemic of *gal khotu* was then raging and people were dying everywhere. There really was no treatment for *gal khotu* except that your father was expected to convince healthy people to keep away from the sick. But how could people do that? They lived in such close quarters. Mothers had to look after their children. Families could not desert their sick, though, believe me, some did, so terrified was the public. Anyway, your father's boss was an Englishman by the name of Dr. McCann. Your father learned a lot from Dr. McCann and Dr. McCann sent many good reports of your father to the head office. The McCanns lived up the road from us in one of those big houses with large gardens built for *sahib log*. In the evenings, Mrs. McCann walked down the road with a stick and her dog. Sometimes I would be outside the house running after your brother Sadiq, who was about three then and very active, and Mrs. McCann would stop and say *'salam, kaya hal he'*. She would point at Sadiq and say *'acha bacha'*. She was very nice."

"What else did she say?" I asked.

"Not much. How could she? She only knew a few words of Urdu, though your father told me that Dr. McCann's Urdu was much better. Many English people had *munshis* to teach them Urdu. The McCanns had many guava trees in their garden and in season Mrs. McCann sometimes sent guavas to us via her servant."

"Did she send any *mathai*?" I asked mischievously.

"No," my mother laughed. "The English did not like our *mathais*. It is too sweet for them."

"Did you ever go to the McCanns' house?"

"No, no, no," my mother said, surprised, not expecting such strange question. "They had their own friends, other white people. Sometimes I saw them through the gate, eating and drinking."

"Did they drink *shirab*?" I asked mischievously again.

"How would I know what they drank? They probably did drink *shirab*, and ate pig's meat, too. These things are not prohibited to the Christians, you know."

"Who else lived in the house?" I asked.

"Just the two of them, Dr. and Mrs. McCann. Servants lived in the servant's quarters in the back."

"Did they not have any children?"

"They were much older than your father and I. I think they had children but they were back in England. English people sent their children to school in England and they stayed there and only returned to India if they wanted jobs here, in the Civil Service or the army. I expect Dr. and Mrs. McCann eventually retired to England."

Once, when I was living in England, I went to see my mother in Lahore. My father had died and my mother was living with one of my brothers.

"Mother," I said, "you know what? I was invited by the Queen to her house."

"*Malka e Hind* , you mean?" she said, utterly surprised.

"No, mother, she is no longer *Malka* of Hindustan. We are independent now."

"I know. I know. Why were you, a poor student, invited?"

"Well, she invited all the Rhodes Scholars who were at Oxford, along with some other people."

"Is she related to *Malka* Victoria?"

"Yes, I think so, perhaps her great-great-granddaughter," I said.

"You really mean you went to her house? It must be a big palace."

"Yes, it is big. Like the Red Fort in Delhi. It is called the Buckingham Palace."

"And did she talk to you?"

"She said hello and asked how I was doing. As I said, there were many other people."

"Has she any children?"

"Yes, but they were not at the party. They may not be living at home."

"I know. The English don't keep children at home for long. They send them to the boarding schools. Your father insisted on sending your older brother, Sadiq, to a boarding school once. He thought the education was better there but I missed him greatly."

My mother wanted to know everything about my encounter with the *Malka*.

So I told her. "I went by train to London," I said, "and got off at a station called Paddington Station and hailed a taxi. 'Where do you want to go?' asked the *taxiwalla*. 'Buckingham Palace,' I said. 'Where near Buckingham Palace?' he asked, thinking I was using Buckingham Palace as some kind of reference point. 'To Buckingham Palace itself,' I said, deadpan. 'Private entrance,' I added for extra effect. I tell you, mother, I could have scraped that *taxiwalla* off the ground. Those *taxiwallas* in London think we are know-nothing foreigners. Anyway, when we reached the palace, I showed the invitation card at the gate, and the gatekeeper politely waved the taxi in."

My mother put her arms around me. "I remember when you were a little boy running around the house," she said. "How could I ever imagine you would be invited by the *Malka* to her palace?" Then, after a pause, she said, "I always thought *angrezi log* were very kind. They did so much for us. Built canals, railways, hospitals. Above all, for the first time, we had peace in the country. And how did we show our gratitude? We treated them shabbily and forced them out of India. And, look, they are still good to us. Their *Malka* invited you to her palace. I think *angrez* are Allah's special people."

I looked at her. She was wiping tears with her *dopatta*.

14

The summer of 1946 was the last peaceful summer in Mukerian, and the people talked of nothing but the coming independence and the political machinations in the country. This was new as ordinary Indians usually paid little attention to national politics. They had never played any part in the governance of their country which was all carried out in far-off places. The small talk had always been of heat, too much or too little rain, shortages of staples like wheat and sugar, and family illnesses and deaths. True, in school we occasionally sang songs of patriotism and lamented that the Indians were still slaves to a foreign power, but up to this time it hardly bothered the population at large who had always lived under an autocracy of one kind or another.

Jinnah was now the dominant figure among the Muslims, and among the Muslims he alone called the tune. They called him *Quaid-e-Azam*, the Great Leader. His hold on the Muslims, especially the young, was complete. He had convinced them that in a united independent India, they would have to live under the Hindu yoke. In the summer of 1946 my brother Bashir came home from the university for his summer vacation. He had seen and heard Jinnah and was swept up in the enthusiasm for a Muslim homeland. "Gandhi is a wolf in sheep's clothing," Bashir said, "and remember that he is a *bania*," and he quoted a common Punjabi saying; "three things you can never trust even when they are asleep: a dog, a crow and a *bania*." Those who have not seen the Indian crows may not appreciate the significance of this saying, but a sleepy-looking Indian crow can suddenly swoop down and grab the food right off your plate and, as for the *banias*, they were the traditional traders and moneylenders in India and they were often accused of being devious and always looking for a bargain. "Gandhi is trying to be nice to the Muslims but he is waiting for the British to leave." Bashir and my father had long discussions. "I have worked with the Hindus all my life," my father said. "I do not find them any more devious than the Muslims. If they are richer than Muslims, it is because they are enterprising and work hard." Curiously, Bashir, though so enamoured with Jinnah and the idea of Pakistan, never practiced his religion; never went to the mosque, prayed, read the Quran, or observed Ramadan. Perhaps in this respect he was no different from Jinnah himself. Bashir, like many Muslims, suspected that after independence the Congress Party would assume the agenda of the *Hindu Mahasabha*.

My father was worried, not so much that Bashir had accepted Jinnah's political philosophy, which seemed to be almost the norm among the Muslim youth then, but that Bashir had also joined a militant Muslim movement called *Tehrik-e-khaksar*. *Tehrik-e-khaksar* promoted itself as the strong arm of Muslims in India. The *Tehrik* had been started in early 1930s by a man name Inayatullah Khan who assumed the rather grand title of *Allama Mashriqi*, the 'Wise man of the East'. Inayatullah had studied at Cambridge, where, according to *Tehrik's* propaganda, he set unmatched records of academic excellence. The *Tehrik* was loosely based on the Brownshirts and the Blackshirts of Europe. In fact, *Allama Mashriqi* claimed to have met Hitler and there is little doubt that Inayatullah, like Subhash Chander Bose, was impressed by the trappings of Nazi grandeur. *Khaksars*, *Tehrik's* followers, were the 'Muslim Stormtroopers'. Dressed in brown shirts and brown shorts, each carried a *belcha*. The *belchas* were surrogates for the guns which in those days were not readily available. *Khaksars* spent much of their time in camps and on the parade grounds where they were expected to build 'martial character'. *Allama Mashriqi* constantly talked of, and wrote about, the old days of Muslim glory, the glitter of Baghdad and Granada, and the days of Muslim rule in India. *Allama Mashriqi* was opposed to the partition of Punjab and felt that Delhi, as the old seat of Muslim power, should be part of Pakistan. At its height, the *Tehrik* claimed to have over four million members, no doubt a wild exaggeration. The British were wary of *Allama Mashriqi*, as they were of Bose, and put him under house arrest in Southern India. The exuberant, youthful *Khaksars* clashed with the police in Lahore, resulting in many casualties. *Tehrik* was soon sidelined by Jinnah's juggernaut. Autocratic Jinnah, already the 'Great Leader' brooked no 'Wise Man of the East'.

Realizing that independence was coming and time was of the essence, Jinnah declared August 16, 1946, a 'Direct Action Day'. Jinnah was probably taking a cue from Gandhi who with his *satyagrahas* and *hartals* had often brought the government to its knees. The idea, as we understood it, was that on the Direct Action Day, Muslims would not go to work, would close their shops, and hold public meetings where the idea of Pakistan would be promoted by Muslim League speakers. In Mukerian, Muslims, as Jinnah decreed, shut down their shops that day. The schools were closed for the summer vacation anyway. A meeting was organized by the local Muslim League but no one from our family went to the meeting for fear of violence. The day however passed peacefully. But the news we heard in the coming days was not good. In Calcutta, there were brutal fights between Hindus and Muslims with thousands killed. Over the next few days there was a steady stream of bad news. Riots spread to other cities in Bengal and Behar but the Punjab remained calm. Though shocking at the time, the mindless savagery was only a foretaste of what was to come later in the Punjab.

From now on, my father's friends began to gather with much greater regularity, and Rafiq and I made sure we were there to listen to the latest news and rumours. Ramzan was the preeminent source of the news as he now had a radio at home, and we did not have to wait till the following day for the daily The Civil & Military Gazette[12]. We would all sit and wait with bated breath for Ramzan, who, as always, was dutifully followed by his *hookahbardar*. Who had started the riots on the Direct Action Day was debated. As always, Hindus had blamed Muslims, Muslims had blamed Hindus, and both were blaming the British. My father's friends, being of diverse religions, and respectful of each other, blamed the *goondas* and *badmashes*. The events in Bengal and Behar did not seem to unsettle people in Mukerian. Bengal and Behar were far off, and there was a feeling that Punjab was different. "We Punjabis know how to live together," people were saying. "We are not emotional like those Bengalis." It is chilling to remember those remarks now, considering what happened in the Punjab before the year was out.

15

It may seem strange but the first stirring of religious unrest in Mukerian started at our school. It was a government school, not sectarian or denominational. It was true that most of the staff, including Headmaster Bhalla, were Hindu, but then Mukerian was predominantly Hindu, and even in areas where

Muslims were in majority, Hindus had disproportionate share of positions in the public institutions.

Though we never encountered any overt Hindu teaching at the school, the Muslims in Mukerian, perhaps encouraged by Muslim Leaguers, began talking about starting a separate Muslim school. In principle, it might not have been a bad idea but in that charged atmosphere the timing was terrible. However, within a few months a small site had been found and enrollment was launched with much fanfare. Inevitably, it caused difficulties between Muslim and Hindu families. "If you are a Muslim it is your duty to enroll your child in the Muslim school," was the line advanced by the founders of the new school, though the Muslim school had hardly proper physical facilities, let alone any staff. Muslim parents were under pressure to enroll their children in the Muslim school. My father said that Rafiq and I must continue in the A.S. High School. This decision caused no problem for Rafiq, for he was in the last year of his school and the Muslim school was not yet ready to take students at that level. But it was different with me as the Muslim school was enrolling students in my grade. I had both Muslim and Hindu friends in school. Amrit, my neighbour and a Hindu, was my best friend. As more and more Muslim students defected to the Muslim school, I was put in a most uncomfortable position. My father, insensitive as he was to religious 'clap-trap', saw no problem. My mother who realized how uncomfortable I was feeling, tried to persuade my father to change his mind and let me enroll in the Muslim school but he refused. He even went to Headmaster Bhalla to tell him the he intended to keep his sons in the A.S. High School. Headmaster Bhalla, who was desperate to show that his school still commanded allegiance of both Hindus and Muslims, was very pleased with my father's decision[13]. Dr. Husain had no qualms about moving his son to the Muslim school. Latterly, he had started coming to see my father on Sunday mornings. Sunday was a slow day at the hospital and my father was often at home. These visits on Sundays allowed

Dr. Husain to talk to my father without the presence of any Hindu or Sikh.

"Doctor Sahib," Dr. Husain said, "you are making a mistake by keeping your children in the A.S. High School. You know there is scarcely a Muslim teacher there. In the Muslim school we can teach religion and Islamic point of view."

"I do not see any reason to send them to the Muslim school," my father replied. "Schools are for learning subjects like math and English, not for teaching religion. We teach religion at home."

"But, Doctor Sahib, you don't do that at home. You have not even taught the Quran to your children. In the Muslim school they will have an opportunity to read the Quran which, as you know, they will never have in A.S. High School."

"I can't teach the Quran to my children because I can't read it myself. I never learned to read Arabic, you know."

"You can arrange a *qari* to come and teach them at home," advised Muhammad Husain.

"Yes, I suppose I can," my father said resignedly, but no *qari* ever came.

16

"We have a new Viceroy," announced Ramzan one evening. "Wavell is leaving and a new fellow, Mountbatten, is coming."

There was not much surprise or excitement. "One *Laat Sahib* is the same as another," said Ravi contemptuously. To him all British were foreign conquerors and it was immaterial who their nominal head in India was.

Soon after his arrival, Mountbatten announced that the British would leave India by June 1948. Even the diehard nationalists were now convinced that this time the British were serious and really meant to leave India. In school, we stopped singing patriotic songs calling on Indian youth to fight for independence. Those songs were redundant now. It was obvious to all that the real issue now was not the struggle for power between the British and the Indians, but the struggle for power between Hindus and Muslims, with Sikhs complicating the situation in the Punjab. The patriotic songs in the school denouncing the British were replaced by songs promoting Hindu-Muslim unity like *Hindu-Muslim bhai bhai*.

More and more political speakers now came to Mukerian. Most of them were still the *Congresswallas*, who supported Gandhi's demand for a united independent India, but there were now Muslim Leaguers, too. The Unionist Party was still ruling the Punjab but it was a ghost of its former self, bereft of power as most of its Muslim members had defected to the Muslim League.

"The Unionist Party is just a creation of the British and now that the British are leaving, what purpose can it serve?" said Ravi one day, looking at Ramzan.

"But you have to admit, Ravi, that it kept Hindu, Muslim and Sikhs united," replied Ramzan.

"Well, Hindu, Muslim, and Sikh are united under the Congress Party. The Congress Party stands for everyone, even for the *achoot*," said Ravi.

"It is one thing to talk of independence, but what is this talk about partition and the creation of two countries?" asked Joginder.

"It won't happen, and even if it does, so what? Punjab will stay united. We are not going to be affected," my father said.

"That is for sure," agreed Joginder.

It seems that as late as spring of 1947 no one around us took the idea of Pakistan seriously, certainly not as an independent country. It either meant some kind of separate electorate for the Muslims with guaranteed seats in the provincial and federal parliaments or, what was now looking more likely, a semiautonomous part of India. If the permanent partition of India seemed to us unlikely, the permanent partition of Punjab was unthinkable. The three religious groups in Punjab, Muslims, Hindus, and Sikhs, were so integrated that few could think of a divided Punjab.

There was now constant talk of round-table meetings of Hindu, Muslim, Sikh, and British leaders. I imagined, correctly I suppose, that they were sitting around a big round table to make sure that they all felt equal. Most ordinary people did not understand what was going on at those round tables. So many rumours were flying around and all of them were heavily varnished by the Muslim League and the Congress to serve their respective demands.

17

One Sunday morning, Dr. Husain said to my father. "This fellow Gandhi. Do you really trust him?"

"I think he is sincere but I don't understand why he has been agitating for independence. We are just out of a war. Can't we sit back and have a few years of peace? Civil disobedience is never civil, as we know. It always ends in a *lathi charge*, if not firing, and the injured end up here in the hospital," my father said.

"Independence is now coming anyway," said Muhammad Husain. "The British have announced that. I am now worried about the future for Muslims in India. Now it looks like the Punjab is going to be divided and we here in Mukerian will be India. I think it will be better for us Muslims in Pakistan."

"Your family and mine have lived in Punjab for centuries. Our people saw the Mughal rule, the Sikh rule, and the British rule. Rulers come and go but our lives go on," my father said gravely. "I have bought a lot in Dasuya to build my retirement home. I am not going anywhere."

Dr. Husain was not convinced. "But Jinnah is right. In an independent India we will be dominated by the Hindus," he said.

"That is because they are smarter than Muslims," replied my father. "Hindus are more interested in education and so they do well. Whenever I have a choice I send my sons to a Hindu rather than a Muslim school. Here in Mukerian, the school staff is mostly Hindu and we have a Hindu headmaster. I am happy with the school and have no intention of sending my children to the new Muslim school."

In my father's simplistic view you rose as high as your abilities allowed. That was why British were at the top and the Muslims at the bottom. I am sure that, like his friends, my father never thought of the Untouchables. Rafiq and I often went to the bazaar to shop for my mother. We made a short cut to the bazaar through the Untouchable *basti*. Harya, one of the *chamars*, was employed at the hospital and, as we passed by his hut, we said hello to his family but we were not expected to stop and socialize with them, and they never asked us to do so, though Harya was one of our good servants.

As I said, *Hindu-Muslim bhai bhai* had now largely replaced *Jai Hind*. The *Congresswallas* were aggressively attacking Jinnah personally: "Jinnah does not even know how to say his prayers," "Jinnah is not a real Muslim," "Jinnah loves scotch and eats pork." They even told jokes about him, how, for example, Jinnah was once persuaded to go to the mosque and did not even know how to say his prayers. Muslim Leaguers had their own slogans. They tried to ridicule Gandhi with his goat and his *"Ram Ram mantras."* They tried to convince Muslims that Gandhi was insincere and that in his heart Gandhi wanted an *Akhand Bharat*.

18

Events were now moving fast. Indian independence, originally slated for the middle of 1948, was now moved forward to the middle of 1947. Even now our family and friends did not take seriously the concept of a permanent independent Pakistan. Pakistan, we thought, would be part of a greater India. There would be so many Hindus in the Muslim-majority Pakistan, and so many Muslims in the Hindu-majority India that nobody would dare persecute the minorities. This was the so-called 'hostage theory', believed by many, including Jinnah.

It assumed certain logic on the part of the population, an assumption which was to prove so disastrously wrong. Also, people in the Punjab were still clinging to the hope that Punjab would remain undivided. Jinnah originally wanted the whole of Punjab to be part of Pakistan. When he was outmaneuvered, partly because the Sikhs refused to join him, he had no option but to accept the partition of Punjab, the East Punjab (Hindu and Sikh majority) and the West Punjab (Muslim majority). The exact boundary was not going to be announced until after independence but the general outlines of the two parts were beginning to be clear. Mukerian was no doubt going to be in India.

19

The summer of 1947 arrived early and by the end of April the temperature was soaring to 45C day after day. The sun beat down relentlessly. Some said afterwards that they saw blood spots on the moon, others that they heard strange howling noises at night. Yet others claimed they saw an unusually large number of vultures flying high in the sky. Such portents, presaging calamities, were not new:

> In the most high and palmy state of Rome,
> A little ere the mightiest Julius fell,
> The graves stood tenantless, and the sheeted dead
> Did squeak and gibber in the Roman streets
> . . . and the moist star,
> Upon whose influence Neptune's empire stands,
> Was sick almost to doomsday with eclipse.

By May, a steady stream of wounded, injured by knives, swords, spears, and *lathis*, started arriving at the hospital from surrounding villages. The news from the rest of Punjab was even worse. Mukerian itself was still calm, the bazaar was busy, and the people went about their business as usual. Uncle Jamil came to visit us from Dasuya. He was the patriarch of one branch of our family and owned a business in Dasuya with his two younger brothers, Hanif and Abdur Rehman. All three brothers, with their large families, lived in a Muslim *muhalla* of Dasuya. It was the same *muhalla* where my father had bought a plot of land to build his retirement home. My oldest brother Sadiq, who was away in Burma with the Indian Army, was engaged to one of Jamil's daughters. Jamil was worried about the security situation and wanted to discuss the options with my father. Should they leave Dasuya temporarily and move to Lahore? "I am going to Lahore for a wedding and I can arrange temporary accommodation there for the families," he said. We were certain that Lahore was going to be safe for the Muslims. My father played down Jamil's fears with his usual comments, "The situation will calm down after independence," he said. "After all, if the country is divided, there will be huge minorities on each sides of the border. How can they all leave?"

The opinions of my father's friends had hardened noticeably, but the camaraderie remained. It was likely that in private they all, like Muhammad Husain, were beginning to form opinions which they were reluctant to share with friends of other religions. Was our family in physical danger? Pandit Bansi Lal could not imagine anything serious happening to us. "You are respected and loved by all," he said to my father. "Who would want to harm you?" His opinion was not entirely unfounded. My father worked hard to look after his patients, and he did this without any consideration of religion or people's ability to pay. He was well-known in the area for his 'healing touch' which meant a lot to simple Indian people. He had done hundreds of cataract operations on the elderly and had successfully persuaded local businessmen to start a fund to buy glasses for patients after their cataract operation. In fact, my father's patients had nicknamed him *chota paramatma*, to distinguish him from *bara paramatma* high above. I had seen patients and their relatives literally kissing his feet in gratitude. Perhaps my father, too, felt in his heart that, whatever the circumstances, he would not be harmed.

He had every intention of staying in Mukerian, come what may.

The Unionist Party of Sir Khizar Hayat collapsed early in 1947, and the governor Sir Evan Jenkins assumed the control of the province. Relations between Sikhs and Muslims became very testy. Now we increasingly heard the name of the Sikh leader, Tara Singh (he was commonly called Master Tara Singh because he started his career as a school master). Tara Singh was soon to become the person most hated by the Muslims.

In early June the news came that Punjab, as well as Bengal, were going to be divided between India and Pakistan, and that the division had been accepted by leaders of all the parties. The news was devastating to all, Hindus, Muslims, and Sikhs. Muslims had hoped that all of the Punjab would be included in Pakistan; after all, the first letter of Pakistan stood for the Punjab. Hindus and Sikhs had hoped that whole of the Punjab would be part of India. Punjab and Bengal were the two most populous provinces of India, whose inhabitants, though of different religions, were nevertheless well-integrated. Each province had a distinct language, Punjabi and Bengali. Throughout the vicissitudes of history, Bengal and Punjab had more or less retained their integrity.

All the government employees in Punjab were now asked by the provincial government if they wanted to be in India or Pakistan. The government was offering to transfer them if, because of their religion, they were going to be on the wrong side of the border, though the exact border had not yet been defined. I remember Dr. Husain came to see my father one morning. He, too, had received the government letter and had decided to opt for Pakistan. He and my father had a long conversation. Dr. Husain tried to persuade my father to opt for Pakistan too. "The partition will not be permanent," Dr. Husain said. "We can always come back when the turmoil is over." But my father refused to change his mind. "It is no different from the other catastrophes, like famines and plagues that we have suffered before. We survived those and we will survive this, too. After all, my family has lived here for centuries." This had now become his standard answer whenever any Muslim asked his opinion.

20

Of our friends, Joginder Singh was now totally occupied with the political affairs of the Sikh community. Joginder was the most prominent local Sikh and was now the head of the local *Akali Dal*, the main Sikh political party in Punjab. Originally formed to take control of the financially lucrative gurdwaras, *Akali Dal* had become, under Tara Singh, a party which was determined to look after the Sikh interests at *any* cost. It had tried to lobby Britain to keep Punjab as one province under Sikh dominance, just as it was before the British annexed it in 1849. British had always been sympathetic to the Sikhs. After all, the Sikhs provided vital support to the British during the Indian Mutiny of 1857. They also provided large number of soldiers to the British-Indian army. Some Sikhs even dreamt, and still do, of forming an entirely independent state of Khalistan. All this had failed, and the Punjab was now going to be divided. Their dreams shattered, the Sikhs were furious.

It seemed obvious that there would be more trouble in Punjab, and the trouble would largely be between Muslims and Sikhs. Hindus, though annoyed with Muslims for demanding Pakistan and rupturing Indian unity, were not as incensed with Muslims as the Sikhs were. Unlike Sikhs, Hindus were not out for Muslim blood, though they were willing to sit back and watch the Muslim slaughter with some satisfaction. Though everyone predicted violence between Sikhs and Muslims, nobody could have remotely foreseen the extent of it. Nor could anyone have imagined the wholesale transfer of populations between the two, yet to be born, countries. We were beginning to hear rumours that *Akalis* were well organized and had formed armed *jathas*. Their gurdwaras, including the Golden Temple at Amritsar, were both houses of worship and military headquarters[14]. Also, the Sikh Princely States provided sanctuary where the Sikhs could train, and retreat if needed. This did not mean that the Muslims were sitting idly by. The Muslim League had also formed a small, though less armed, paramilitary organization called the Muslim League Guards. Muslims, though unhappy with the partition of Punjab, were not as bitter as the Sikhs, but they were fully prepared to slaughter Sikhs if necessary.

Tara Singh now made a highly provocative speech. "Oh, Sikhs," shouted Tara Singh. "Know ye that our brethren are threatened by those who call us infidels. Our lands are about to be overrun, our women dishonored and our children forced to take alien vows. It is time for our warriors to arise and once more destroy the Mughal invader. Revenge our people! Spare no one who stands in the way of Sikh rights in our land" (quoted by Mosley). This was March 4, 1947, and Tara Singh, brandishing an unsheathed sword, was standing in front of the Punjab Assembly Chamber, an impressive building in the centre of Lahore with Queen Victoria's statue in front (it has since been replaced by a Quran), calling for Muslim blood, and raising Sikhism old martial slogan: *"Raj karega Khalsa, baqi rahe na koi"* (Only the Sikhs will rule, others will be destroyed). Outraged Muslims started slaughtering Sikhs in Lahore. Sikhs responded with equal brutality. In the Sikh city of Amritsar, Sikhs captured Muslim women, paraded them naked in the bazaar, and then raped and killed them. Police refused to intervene everywhere and in some cases actually helped their coreligionists.

As horrible stories of Sikhs being butchered in Lahore and Rawalpindi began to circulate in Mukerian, Sikhs started to retaliate. First there were isolated attacks on individual Muslims but soon news came of more coordinated attacks on Muslim villages, usually at night.

By early July the wounded in our hospital were lying in the open on *charpoys* under the trees. Fortunately, monsoon season had not yet started, though the heat was unbearable and flies were buzzing mercilessly. In Mukerian, almost all the injured, as expected, were Muslims.

It was about this time that a small contingent of the Indian army arrived and camped outside Mukerian. The contingent was under the command of a Hindu, Major Bhagwan Das. A kindly man, Major Bhagwan Das and my father quickly became friends; their friendship was further cemented by the fact that Major Bhagwan Das and one of my father's cousins had served together on the Burma front. Major Sahib occasionally came in the evening to join our circle of friends, though most of the time he was busy reconnoitering the villages to keep the violence down. With his pathetically small number of soldiers, Major Sahib was responsible for keeping peace in hundreds of villages. Nonetheless, as private guns were uncommon and most of the killing was done with knives, swords and spears, one armed soldier could put the fear of God into a large group of marauders. Occasionally, my father took me on the back of his bicycle to visit Major Bhagwan Das at his army camp. Once, Major Sahib took us on a sightseeing trip to the nearby hills in his jeep. A few weeks later a distinct Boundary Defense Force (BDF) was created to control violence along the line of partition. The BDF, though highly effective in saving thousands of lives, was nonetheless too little too late.

We were now getting visits from our relatives and friends who lived in Mirpur and other nearby villages and who looked to my father for guidance. If anybody had a finger on the pulse, they reasoned, it had to be my father who was not only a respectable member of the community but, through Major Bhagwan Das, had contact with the Indian army. Mirpur had not been attacked but some surrounding villages had been raided by Sikhs at night and a number of people had been killed. Uncle Jamil had gone to Lahore for the wedding. Though he was personally safe in Lahore, which soon became an important city of Pakistan, he had to watch, agonizingly, the events unfolding back home. Hanif and Abdul Rehman came to visit us and discussed the situation further. Dasuya was now suffering minor violence and some Muslims had been killed. My father once again counselled patience.

One day, Dr. Husain came to see us. He was leaving for Pakistan. He had opted for Pakistan, and his transfer orders had arrived. "I have cast my lot with India, Muhammad Husain," my father said to him. "We have lived here for centuries and we are not going anywhere." They embraced tearfully, and Dr. Husain was gone[15].

Though my father was still certain that the communal violence would pass, he did make half-hearted attempts to prepare for an emergency in case some misguided person tried to harm us. His decision to prepare was precipitated by an event, which, though disturbing at the time, was soon forgotten. We were eating at home in the evening when someone started shouting outside our door. "Doctor. You *manchod*. We know all about you. We are going to get you and other Muslims, you traitors." My father ordered us all to stay put and keep quiet. A couple of minutes later, Bansi Lal, who could hear it all from his house next door, came out and persuaded the ruffian to leave. "The man was crazy. Don't take him seriously," said Bansi Lal, visibly embarrassed because the man shouting the obscenities was a Hindu. "You are right, Bansi Lal. There are strange people everywhere," my father added consolingly.

My father possessed an old sword, given to him as a souvenir by a grateful patient. The sword was sent to the local blacksmith for sharpening. My father also obtained, I don't know from where, two bottles of sulfuric acid. He then gathered us around him and gave instructions. "If our house is attacked, go upstairs. From there, climb the temporary bamboo ladder to the roof of the upstairs room. Once you are on the roof of that room, pull the ladder up. If the attackers break the front door and enter the house, throw acid on them from above and shout loudly to Bansi Lal for help." He did not say anything about the sword, perhaps thinking that none of us would have the ability to use it. Our preparations were complete!

21

The visits from our relatives and friends became more frequent, and there was now a sense of urgency and desperation about them. My father's answer remained the same to the very end. "I have both Hindu and Sikh friends and they assure me that this religious animosity is not going to last. Once India gets its independence, people will quietly go back to their daily work. There will no longer be any need for *jalsa* or *jaloose*, where politicians get their opportunity to incite people to violence."

Much has been written about the great "tryst with destiny" speech which Nehru delivered on August 14. Nehru's speech went largely unnoticed in Mukerian. Hardly anyone, except Ramzan, had a radio, and most people were illiterate and could not read the newspapers the following day. The speech was directed at Western audience, not Indians. What was more important to the people in Mukerian and the rest of the Punjab was the boundary line which was going to be drawn across Punjab. This line, dividing India and Pakistan, which was a matter of life and death to thousands of people, was not going to be announced until after independence, so as not to mar the independence celebrations which Mountbatten wanted so much to enjoy. Hundreds of thousands of people, therefore, woke up on the day after independence not knowing whether they were Indians or Pakistanis!

Clement Attlee, the British Prime Minister, had asked a British lawyer, Cyril Radcliffe, to draw the boundary between India and Pakistan. We more or less knew that our district of Hoshiarpur would be part of India, but so much else was subject of intense speculation. Ravi, for example, was still hoping that Lahore would go to India. The Muslims in Mukerian were fairly certain that the boundary line near Mukerian would be the river Beas which was only about four miles from Mukerian. This was reassuring, for if worse came to worst, the Muslims of Mukerian had only to cross the river to enter Pakistan.

I remember well the evening when we learned the details of the Radcliffe Award. It was getting dark when Ramzan came to tell us what he had heard on the radio. Lahore was given to Pakistan but most of the District of Gurdaspur had been awarded to India, The details of the partition line in Bengal really meant little to us. Award of Gurdaspur to India was of immediate interest as it meant that even if we crossed the river Beas we would still be in hostile Indian territory.

22

In early August there were serious riots in Dasuya with many Muslims killed. Uncle Hanif came to see my father yet again and said that the families of all my three uncles in Dasuya were thinking of temporarily moving to Lahore. As I said, Uncle Jamil was already in Lahore.

"We are convinced that that situation is going to get worse in the next few weeks, even if it eventually gets better," Uncle Hanif said. "We talk to a lot of people who do business with us in Dasuya. The Sikhs are very angry with the Muslims. They tell lurid tales of how Sikhs are being slaughtered in Rawalpindi and Lahore. One Sikh told me that Muslims first rape Sikh women, then cut off their men's penises and ram them down their women's throats, and then slaughter them all. I don't know how much of this is true but Sikhs believe it all, and more. They say that Master Tara Singh has told them to kill Muslims wherever they find them. Some of our Hindu friends have advised us to shut the shop and go to Pakistan, and wait there till the communal violence has cooled down. They have even promised to guard our property while we are away."

During the next day or two there were interminable discussions in our house. My father invited Joginder Singh and introduced him to Uncle Hanif. "If anyone can give us good advice it is Joginder," my father said to Uncle Hanif as they sat down for a prolonged meeting. Joginder said, "The

Sikhs are responding here and there to avenge the barbarities committed on them by the Muslims in Pakistan. We, the Sikh leaders, are doing our best to control our community."

"Do you think we should send our families to Pakistan in the meantime?" my father asked Joginder.

Joginder looked at my father and said "I don't see any danger for your family here in Mukerian, Doctor Sahib. But as for other Muslims, I really cannot give any advice. I know we Sikhs are by nature peaceful unless really provoked," he added. If Joginder's description of atrocities committed by Muslims in Lahore and Rawalpindi was true, what more did the Sikhs need to be "really provoked"? What Joginder was saying was what every religious community leader was saying: "We are good people and never start a fight, but if provoked, by God, we will strike back and annihilate our enemies." The problem with this line of reasoning was obvious: no community was ever going to admit, nor has one ever admitted, that it was the first to strike.

My father respected Joginder's opinion. There was no doubt that Joginder, being the leader of the local *Akalis,* knew more about the Sikh feelings and of *Akali* plans than anyone else. But was Joginder telling the truth? Did he know more than he was letting on?

My father consulted other friends, including Bansi Lal and Ravi Saroop. They were not close to the Sikh community and did not know much more than my father. Though they tried to reassure my father, they saw wisdom in the suggestion that it would be safer for our family to temporarily move to Pakistan until the trouble blew over. We could stay in Lahore with Uncle Jamil's friends or go to Lyallpur where we had some relatives and where my brother Bashir was studying. My father said categorically that he himself was not prepared to leave the hospital unattended. "I am the only doctor in town. How can I leave?" he said. But he now agreed to send his family, with the families of my uncles in Dasuya, to Pakistan. My sister Hamida wanted to stay with my father to look after him, which we all thought was a good idea.

So it was decided that the families in Dasuya would pack up and come to our house in Mukerian. From Mukerian we would cross the river Beas in a boat and enter Pakistan, and then safely travel to Lahore. The Radcliffe Line had not yet been announced and we were assuming that the river Beas would be the natural boundary between India and Pakistan.

23

I cannot remember on which day the families from Dasuya arrived at our house. It must have been a day or two after August 17 because they were not there the day Ramzan brought the news of the Radcliffe Award and we learned that river Beas was not going to form the boundary.

With the arrival of our relatives our domestic routines changed drastically. The families of my three uncles comprised about twenty people. Women mostly spent the day cooking on the one *chulla*. There was only one primitive toilet which had to be cleaned repeatedly during the day by the hospital *mehtar*. I saw my mother going around the toilet and kitchen with a *Flit gun* to control the flies. The heat was truly ferocious. The hot weather had one advantage, though; the men and children could spend the day outside under the trees, though the women had to stay indoors. Also, in hot weather we did not need much clothing or bedding.

The adult men in the house spent most of the day discussing the best route to Pakistan. Though after the Radcliffe Award, the river Beas was no longer the boundary between India and Pakistan, this route was not yet rejected. This route was still shorter than the train route via Jalandhar. The adults went over the NWR (North-Western Railway) timetable again and again, not quite realizing that the train system in Punjab had already been seriously disrupted.

Since the beginning of August, more and more Muslims were coming to see my father and seeking his opinion. Extra chairs and *charpoys* were placed under the tree. Dr. Husain had already left for Pakistan. Joginder Singh was no longer a regular visitor as he was usually away on *Akali* business but occasionally came to see my father at the hospital in the mornings. I think he was no longer comfortable among the increasing number of Muslims, gathering under the tree in the evenings.

After the announcement of the Radcliffe Award, there was incessant talk of the "partition line." Everyone in the bazaar talked about it. There also was a very sudden and marked deterioration of relations between Muslims and Sikhs. More and more wounded Muslims were arriving at the hospital. They were always wounded by *kirpans*, spears and *lathis*. I cannot remember my father ever mentioning a gunshot wound but then it was possible that people who were shot died right away.

"Joginder is very upset with the Radcliffe Award," my father said to us. "He believes that Jinnah and his Muslims have put a dagger in their back. Frankly, I don't blame him. They are getting nothing out of this independence deal. The Golden Temple is in India and Nankana Sahib (birthplace of Guru Nanak, founder of Sikh religion) in Pakistan."

Rumours had begun to circulate that the train journey was not safe. My father once again asked the opinion of his friends. The general feeling was that though after the Radcliffe Award Pakistan was no longer across the river Beas, it was still better to take that route. Joginder Singh, however, strongly advised against this. "It will not be easy to find transportation on the other side of the river," he said. "Go by train. The trains are safe because there are now policemen assigned to protect each train. You will have no problem." My father's Muslim friends, on the other hand, cautioned against the train journey. "We are hearing stories of Muslims being attacked in the trains," they said. Dhari Ram spoke out most vehemently against the train journey "Doctorji," he said, "I hear bad things in the bazaar. I hear Muslims are snatched from the trains and killed. Sikhs are not letting trains reach Pakistan safely. Please don't go anywhere right now. You and your family should stay here. If you do have to go, please don't take the train. Find a safer way." Ramzan suggested that my father should hire a truck with an armed guard, which was easier said than done. There was the feeling, on the other hand, that though some Muslims might have been killed in the trains, a general assault on the train was now unlikely as the police protection had been provided.

In the end, after much to and fro, my father announced the final decision. "Joginder has been travelling up and down the villages between Mukerian and Jalandhar," my father said. "He strongly recommends going by train. In any case, if police are protecting the passengers in trains, then what is there to worry about? With police protection, the trains are probably safer than any other transportation."

Having made that decision, August 23 was selected the day for the journey. According to the NWR timetable, after arriving at Jalandhar, we could expect an evening train to leave for Lahore. If we missed the train to Lahore that evening, we could wait in the railway waiting room. Spending the night in the railway stations was not unusual. The people from the villages often came to the station without knowing when the next train was due.

24

A few days before our departure, Amrit, Rajini, and I were standing under the mango tree. It was mango season and a few mangoes had dropped on the ground. We each picked one up. "Let us go to the *khandaq*," said Rajini. Next to the hospital was the local police station with a parade ground. On one side of the parade ground was a crude trench with stairs going to the bottom. I don't know what it was for, perhaps something to do with the police training. We called it by the local name of *khandaq* and often went and sat inside it. We descended the stairs and sat down and started sucking our mangoes.

"We hear you are going to Lahore," said Rajini.

"Yes, we are," I said.

"Why are you going?"

"My father thinks it may not be safe to live here. Sikhs are angry with the Muslims. They may attack our house."

"But you can stay in our house," said Rajini.

Sweet Rajini. How little did she know of the adult world! We could not even enter their Brahmin house.

"They are only going for a short time," said Amrit reassuringly. "Doctorji is not going. Once the *angrez* leave, there will be peace." Amrit no doubt had heard that said again and again. After all, that was what Gandhi and other Indian leaders had been saying all along. Amrit did not even know that, officially, *angrez* had already left India on August 14.

We sat there on the floor of the trench for a long time. How fond we had become of each other! Given the opportunity, it was a friendship which could have lasted a lifetime but the adult world was against us. They had written their own script and we had no part in it. Of the three of us in that *khandaq* I was the only one who knew a little of what was going on in the adult world, and that was because I often sat with the adults, not because they wanted me to sit with them, but because they thought me irrelevant, like a pet dog sitting at his master's feet.

25

It was on August 21 or 22 that Dhari saw Rafiq outside our house.

"I hear that doctorji has decided to send his family on the train along with the other relatives," he said.

"Yes, that is the decision. They have consulted the NWR timetable."

"Is doctorji sure it is safe to travel by train?" Dhari asked Rafiq.

"Yes," Rafiq replied. "Joginder Singh thinks it is safe, and now there are police on the train, too. Joginder thinks August 23 is a good day to go."

"I hear big *jathas* have been formed to attack Muslims. There are rumours that even some soldiers from the Patiala state have come to join the *jathas*," Dhari said.

"But we are going by train. How can a *jatha* attack a train protected by police" Rafiq said.

Dhari did not say anything more.

Was Dhari telling Rafiq something we did not know, and something that perhaps he himself was not entirely sure of? Was he questioning the truth of what Joginder Singh was telling my father? Did he fear that a trap might have been laid for us? Rafiq did not tell us about this conversation till many months later in Pakistan. At the time, Rafiq no doubt thought Dhari's comments insignificant. I am sure, though, that even if Rafiq had told my father what Dhari told him, my father would have paid no attention to it. After all, Dhari Ram was only an illiterate servant.

THE CATASTROPHE

I could a tale unfold whose lightest word
Would harrow up thy soul, freeze thy young blood.

Shakespeare

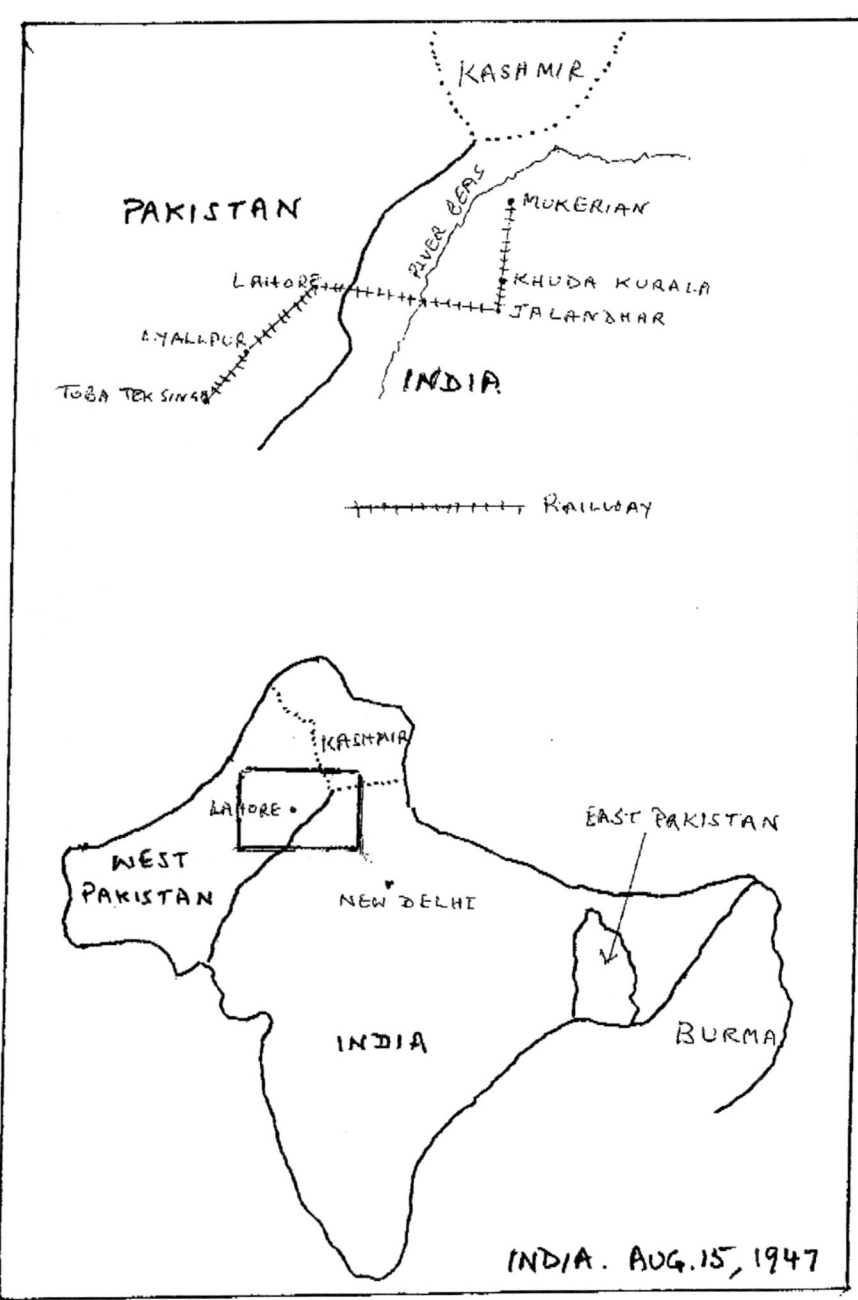

A Refugee Train in India, 1947

A Deserted Street in India with Dead Bodies and Vultures. 1947.

1

August 23, 1947, dawned much like any other summer day in Mukerian. The sky was clear and it was already hot early in the morning. We had now about twenty-five people in our house, including women and children. The decision to take the train to Pakistan had been taken and was final.

The morning was hectic, especially for women. They not only had to cook breakfast for everyone but pack some food for the journey too, especially for the children; the adults could wait till we reached the Jalandhar Railway Station, where we planned to spend a few hours before taking the next train to Lahore. The bundles of clothes and other personal belongings had already been packed and were ready to go.

My father decided we should leave home at about noon and walk to the railway station. As I said, he himself was staying behind with sister Hamida to look after him in our absence. In the morning, my father went to the hospital and saw more than usual number of wounded brought in. There was, of course, no ambulance, no proper stretchers. The wounded were carried on *charpoys* or just walked in if they could. The steady stream of the wounded further convinced my father that his decision to send the family to Pakistan was the right one. Joginder Singh came to see him that morning. My father had kept him informed of our plans, and Joginder again assured him of the safety of train travel and wished good luck.

The train was expected to arrive in Mukerian from Jalandhar at 1pm. Mukerian, being the last station on a branch line from Jalandhar, it usually took a couple of hours for the engine to be disconnected, shunted to the reversing platform, and be hooked to the other end of the train.

Most of the luggage was carried by my father's three servants, supervised by Dhari Ram who was most unhappy that we were leaving. "Who is going to harm you here?" he kept asking.

My father came to the station to say goodbye and buy our tickets. As usual, he did not go to the ticket window but went to the station master whom he knew well. He gave the money for the tickets to the station master who then sent a *chaprasi* with the money to the ticket master. It was considered undignified for the local government doctor to line up at the ticket window along with the poor people.

As we waited on the platform, a group of six or seven men and women arrived. They looked Muslim and started talking to us.

"We are from the village Ber Shah, a few miles from Mukerian," they said. "Last night a Sikh *jatha* attacked our village. Many Muslims were killed. Some of us managed to run and hide in the field. We are now leaving for Pakistan."

One woman in the group had a bandage around her arm. "A Sikh tried to hit me with his *kirpan* but I ran. The Sikh did not pursue as he appeared more interested in looting than killing," she said and started to cry.

When my father returned with the tickets, my mother told him what had happened to those people from Ber Shah. "Of course there is trouble here and there," said my father. "That is why our hospital is full. You know what Joginder Singh has been telling us. This very morning he assured me that this train will reach Jalandhar safely. Major Bhagwan Das has said that more army units are coming, and it is only a matter of time before peace is restored and everything is back to normal. Also, the station master tells me that the trains have been moving back and forth between Mukerian and Jalandhar without any problem."

The train was about an hour late coming and very few passengers disembarked. Uncle Hanif spoke to one of them. "How are things between here and Jalandhar?" Hanif asked. "Not good from what I hear," replied the disembarking man, "but I only boarded the train in Dasuya." Dasuya was only the third station from Mukerian and there were six or seven more before the train reached Jalandhar. And, of course, from Jalandhar we were planning to take yet another train to Lahore. Lahore was beginning to look a long way away.

All of us managed to get into one *bogie*.[1] The women were asked to sit towards the back of the carriage, while the men sat near the doors. As the train was about to leave, we saw five uniformed policemen, four Sikh and one Hindu, boarding the train, their long rifles slung over their shoulders. "They are going to guard the train, just in case someone tries to make any trouble," said my mother. The policemen certainly looked impressive and reassuring. Uncle Hanif asked everyone to pray for safe journey.

As the train left, we waved goodbye to my father and our servants. I noticed Dhari Ram was wiping his eyes. "Why should Dhari Ram be so upset?" I said to myself. "After all we are returning soon."

2

Between my family, my three uncles' families, and three or four Muslim friends, there were between twenty-five and thirty people in the carriage. My family included my mother, my two sisters, Majida and Rashida, and my brother Rafiq. Majida, after graduating from the university, was working as a school teacher in a girls' school in Dasuya but was home for summer holidays. Rashida had graduated from a college in Jalandhar and had recently been married to Khursheed, a captain in the Indian Army. As Khursheed's unit was constantly moving around the country, Rashida had come to stay with us in Mukerian for a few months. Of my two brothers, Sadiq was still in Burma, waiting for the Indian army to be brought back home, and Bashir was in his final year of college in Lyallpur and was consequently safe in Pakistan.

There were about twelve or thirteen stations between Mukerian and Jalandhar but only two significant towns, Dasuya and Tanda Urmur. The other stations served no towns; they were there to serve surrounding villages. These small stations were one- or two-room buildings with a single dirt platform; otherwise on both sides of the railway track there were interminable fields of cotton, wheat, and sugarcane. Sometimes you could see a village, wholly built of mud, from the train.

The second station from Mukerian was called Uchi Bassi. As the train stopped at Uchi Bassi, a man, obviously a Muslim, stepped out of the train and started walking away. "Where are you going, you *mooslay*? Come back," shouted someone from the adjacent carriage. "Bring him back," said another loud voice. At this point, one of the Sikh policemen jumped from the train and ran after the man. The man, taken aback, stopped. The policeman made him return to the train. What was going on? The man looked like a regular passenger getting off the train at Uchi Bassi. Why was the policeman bringing him back? Who had shouted *"mooslay"* at the man? A nervous hush fell over our carriage. Rashida looked at my mother and said, "Don't worry, mother. Everything is peaceful." The train moved. Could this be all? We hoped so. Some of us were now praying loudly. One or two opened the Quran and quietly started reading. As the train moved again, we heard a sound, like the report of a gunshot, from the adjacent carriage. What was it all about?

For the next hour or so the train stopped at a number of stations without any incident until it arrived at a very small station called Khuda Kurala. Our blood froze at what we saw. Standing on both sides of the train track were hundreds of Sikhs with spears and unsheathed *kirpans*. No sooner had the train stopped, than they started shouting slogans: *"Raj kare ga Khalsa"* *"Mussalman murdabad"* *"Pakistan murdabad"*. A Sikh started walking on the platform alongside the train shouting repeatedly: "All Hindus and Sikhs come down from the train. *Mooslays* stay in." As our carriage had no one except Muslims, no one got down. Uncle Hanif said, rather unconvincingly, "These Sikhs can't do anything. The policemen will keep them at bay." In a few minutes all the Hindus and Sikhs, perhaps fifty or so, got down from the other carriages and formed a knot on one side of the platform.

The Sikhs resumed shouting their slogans. They waved their swords and stumped their spears on the ground in rhythm with the slogans. Finally, one Sikh policeman, who was supposed to be guarding the train, came up to our carriage. One of our relatives was standing at the carriage door, presumably to assess the situation. Suddenly the policeman pulled him down on to the platform and made a gesture to the Sikhs behind him as if to say, "Here he is. Deal with him as you wish." Immediately a number of Sikhs pounced on him with swords and spears. Then, without saying another word, the policeman entered our carriage, raised his rifle, and started shooting at us.

Pandemonium broke out. There were shrieks. People rushed towards the back of the compartment and fell upon each other. I remember being crushed under a pile of bodies and my mother trying to pull me out saying, "Please don't crush my son." I cannot say how many shots were fired, perhaps eight, perhaps ten. I assume the policeman stopped firing when he ran out of bullets. There were dead and dying on the floor. Blood was everywhere.

Some scenes are frozen in my memory. When the policeman was firing, one of the adults took the courage and rushed towards him and tried to grab his rifle. Unfortunately, he could only grab the bayonet and the policeman shot him point blank. I remember, too, Rafiq's arms around me as I lay under a pile of bodies. He was panting.

Now the policeman left, and three or four Sikhs with *kirpans* entered. My mother stepped up to one of the Sikhs, with both hands raised in supplication, "*Bhai*, why are you killing us?" she asked. "We have done no harm to you." "We know that," replied the Sikh. "Our people had done no harm when they were mercilessly butchered in Lahore and Rawalpindi.

Mooslays put oil on our children and lit them. We are not *maan de bete* if we don't take revenge." "*Pakistan murdabad*," he shouted at the top of his voice, raising his gleaming sword high.

Rashida who was standing next to my mother said to the Sikhs, "But we have nothing to do with Pakistan. We did not even want it created. We have always believed in one Hindustan." Rashida was a striking-looking girl of 20. Two Sikhs now grabbed Rashida, one arm each and told her to come out of the carriage with them. My mother, fearing the worst, grabbed Rashida and tried to stop the Sikhs from taking her. Rashida looked back at my mother. "Don't worry mother, I will be all right," she said. They pulled her down on to the platform and we saw Sikhs with swords and spears gathering around her and walking her away. That was the last we saw of Rashida.

Now, Majida looked at my mother and suggested that we get down, not on the platform side but on the opposite side, presumably because there were fewer Sikhs on this side. So Majida, mother, and I got down on this side. As there was no platform on this side, we had to make a small jump from the lower step outside the carriage door to the dirt ground below. Majida now led us to the next carriage. Incredibly, no Sikh attacked us. Were some of them now busy looting? I saw two or three Sikhs dragging the luggage from our carriage; looting was as important as murder. Or perhaps the Sikhs thought we were Hindus. Adult Hindu and Muslim men were easily distinguishable by their dress, but women wore the same Punjabi dress, and the boys, Hindu or Muslim, wore similar shorts in summer. Rafiq and I had shorts on. We, therefore, were not obviously distinguishable from the Hindus.

There was a lone Hindu sitting on the far side of this carriage as we entered. He was a moderately-built, well-dressed man, perhaps in his thirties. It was possible that he had never left the train when the order was given for Sikhs and Hindus to get down; being a confident Hindu, he might not have felt any need to get down, or perhaps he had just reentered the carriage. We sat down on the other side of the carriage, facing him. He looked at me and said, "You go to A.S. High School, don't you?" It was more of a statement than a question, but instinctively my mother put her hand over my mouth as if to protect me and stop me from answering. Nobody answered his question, for we did not know what to say.

"I am Dharam Pal. I teach at the A.S. High School in Mukerian," he said. "I have seen you in school," he said. "I know you are the doctor's son. I am surprised you people are still alive. I can try and help you," he said, looking at my mother.

"We got down from the next carriage and walked into this one. The Sikhs did not attack us," my mother said cautiously. She really did not know what to say.

"They think you are Hindus getting back in the train," he said. "Someone will soon come and check. They prefer to kill on the platform because otherwise they have to wash the carriages."

"What should we do?" asked Majida

He thought for a moment and then said, "Well, you can pretend you are Hindu. I will tell them that you are Hindu and that I know you from Mukerian." He said it quietly, without emotion.

"Oh, we will be so grateful to you", my mother said, and then looking at Majida, she said, "Majida, we need Hindu names."

Majida was a school teacher and was not short of Hindu names. She quickly produced Hindu names. I know I was Jagan Lal and my mother was Lajwanti. I cannot remember Majida's name.

The people were still being dragged down from the carriages and hacked to pieces, right there. Most were taken out on the platform side but some were jumping on the opposite side, hoping to run for cover in the fields. I saw a Sikh bringing down his *kirpan* on uncle Hanif with both hands. Uncle Hanif instinctively raised his arms to protect him. One of his arms was cut off and dangled by a shred of skin. The Sikh raised his sword again and made a second attempt. This time the sword hit the middle of my uncle's face. Part of his face and skull was detached and hung for a moment from his neck. I remember it had one bulging eye in it. As he fell down, another Sikh stepped up to him and casually thrust his spear into his throat. As he pulled the spear out, Uncle Hanif took one or two final gasps and went still. I also saw Uncle Abdul Rehman. A Sikh said loudly; "Don't kill him. He owns a *keriana* shop in Dasuya. I buy my groceries from him. He is a good man." "No *mader chod Moosla* is good," shouted another Sikh as he put his spear in Abdul Rehman's chest. I also saw Zaibun Nasa, my cousin, covered with blood, standing on the ground just outside the compartment, holding her baby sister in her arms. She was begging the confronting Sikh to spare the baby. The Sikh grabbed the baby, disemboweled her, and led Zaibun Nasa away.

But where was Rafiq? We tried looking out of the windows. At the same time we did not want to make ourselves too obvious to those outside. Majida had seen Rafiq at the back of our carriage before leaving it, and had called out to him to follow us.

We now saw Rafiq stepping down from the carriage. Before a Sikh could raise his sword to kill him, Majida, with remarkable agility, rushed to the door and called out at the top of her voice: "Ram Parshad, come here. Ram Parshad, come here. We have been looking for you." "He is my brother," she said, looking at the Sikhs below. "Ram Parshad did not hear the announcements. He is *bola*." As she shouted she wagged her finger at the Sikhs as if she were confronting rowdy school children. And then she added in English "No! Don't touch him. He is Hindu." Where did she get the energy and this presence of mind? Perhaps the few words of English, though almost certainly not understood, had that extra effect. The Sikhs held back and Rafiq entered our carriage.

But the Sikhs were not wholly satisfied. One of them followed Rafiq into the carriage.

"Are you all Hindus?" he asked.

"Yes," we answered.

"I know them," said Dharam Pal, "they are Hindu. I teach these boys. I am a schoolmaster."

"But we want to check the boys," the Sikh insisted. We all knew what he meant. He wanted to check to see if we were circumcised. This was the standard procedure for identifying Muslim males. Hindus and Sikhs are never circumcised.

"There is no need," said Dharam in a stern voice. 'I know them." The Sikh withdrew.

In hushed tones, Majida now discussed some way of contacting Rashida. She could not be far from the train. Majida thought of asking Dharam Pal to go and look for her. But the problem was that Rashida by now would have been accepted as a Muslim and to contact her would almost certainly have exposed our own precarious situation. So we did nothing.

A Hindu policeman now entered our carriage and sat down next to Dharam Pal.

"All Hindus?" he asked, casually nodding towards us.

"Yes," we said.

The Hindu policeman did not look violent or aggressive. He looked bored. Unlike his Sikh colleagues, he was not walking up and down the platform encouraging and abetting the orgy of bloodletting. Nor, on the other hand, was he interested in doing anything to save the Muslim lives. He sat there with his rifle between his legs, waiting for the train to leave. We could hear the cries of the last remaining Muslims being butchered outside but the Hindu policeman did nothing.

A terrified Muslim woman entered our compartment from the platform side. She had obviously managed to break away from the Sikhs and was desperately trying to seek refuge. As soon as she entered she fell on her face as a chasing Sikh grabbed her ankles and started dragging her out of the carriage. The woman pleadingly looked at my mother.

"Please save me," she cried.

It was a critically dangerous moment for us. My mother knew the woman from Mukerian but doing anything to help her, even giving her a look of recognition, would have been fatal to us.

"Do you know this woman?" the Hindu policeman asked my mother.

"No," my mother replied, shaking her head.

"But she looked at you as if she knew you," said the policeman.

"I don't think so. How would she?" my mother said.

The woman was dragged out by the Sikh and the policeman did not pursue the matter further.

Later, my mother told us that the Muslim woman, her husband and their children, hearing of us leaving for Pakistan, had decided to do the same, though they were not in our carriage. The Muslim woman must have seen my mother, sitting seemingly safe, and made a dash for her. Her husband and children would have been slaughtered by then, in front of her. Years later, once talking to my mother about August 23, which I did not do very often, my mother said to me tearfully, "you know, I cannot get that Muslim woman out of my mind. She has never stopped haunting me. But what could I do? Helping her would have killed us all."

Hindu and Sikh passengers were now returning to the carriages. They had to step over horribly mutilated bodies into pools of blood, but nobody challenged the murderous Sikhs. Perhaps the Hindu and Sikh passengers were relieved to be alive or perhaps they were glad to see the Muslim massacre.

My final memory of the Khudda Kurala railway station is of a young Muslim man running from the train just before the train restarted. It appeared that the man had been hiding under the train and had to make a run for it before the train moved. He tried to make for the nearest crop field. He was chased by a number of Sikhs. The Muslim would have made it to the fields, but the Sikhs had already anticipated such a situation. They had hidden armed men in the fields. A couple of them suddenly appeared with spears in front of the Muslim and killed him.

It was about two hours since the train had arrived at Khuda Kurala. The station was quiet now; the shrieks and moans had died down.

Scenes as the train moved out of the station: Dead bodies lying haphazardly on the ground, some near the train, others near the fields. An occasional arm or leg on its own. A severed head. A dog already on site. A path leading towards a village and on the path a group of armed Sikhs walking with two or three girls. Did I recognize one of the girls? I think I did; she was my cousin Mushtri.

3

The train now continued its journey from Khudda Kurala to Jalandhar. The Hindu policeman once or twice asked us a few questions; perhaps he was not entirely convinced that we were Hindu, but he did not pursue the matter aggressively. At Tanda Urmur station there were a number of Sikhs with buckets of water, which they used to wash the blood from the carriages. We could hear the splashing of water in the adjacent carriage where we had been shot at. Obviously, the plan to massacre was a coordinated one, involving hundreds of people at more than one station.

"Make sure there is no one hiding under the seats or in the *tatis*," shouted someone from the platform to those washing the carriages.

In Jalandhar the train arrived at platform no. 4 or 5, away from the main station building. It was dark and very quiet. The train terminated here and the few people still on the train got down. The Hindu policeman left without saying anything. We did not see the Sikh policemen who probably stayed behind in Khuda Kurala to take their share of the loot.

"Let us go to the platform 1," said Dharam. We crossed over a small metal bridge to reach platform 1. It was well-lit, and here were all the waiting rooms and offices. Dharam suggested that we wait out the night on the platform floor rather than go into one of the waiting rooms. "It is safer in the open," he said. "I will stay with you the rest of the night," he added.

I told my mother that I was desperate to go to the bathroom. She asked Dharam's advice. Dharam said that as it was dangerous to go into the waiting room, I should urinate right there. Rafiq said he wanted to do it, too. So both of us took a few steps away from the others, stood at the edge of the platform and started urinating.

"They killed everyone," Rafiq said as we urinated.

"Yes," I said.

"Uncle Abur Rehman, Uncle Hanif," he said.

"Yes, I saw that," I said.

"I wonder what happened to Rashida."

"I don't know," I said.

We did not cry or show any emotions as we talked of the massacre. Our minds were numb and we were like spectators who had just finished watching a stage play. The trauma would come later and would take its permanent place.

We all sat down for the night on the platform floor under a naked electric bulb hanging from a long cord. Rafiq now told us that he had been hit by a bullet in his left thigh when the policeman first fired at us in the carriage. In the agitation of the following few hours he was able to ignore his injury, but now it had begun to hurt and his wound had started bleeding profusely. Dharam took Rafiq to the stationmaster's room to get help. After some time, the two returned with a bandage wrapped around Rafiq's thigh. Rafiq said that the person who wrapped the bandage wanted to take his shorts off to facilitate bandaging, but Rafiq had to be careful for it would have exposed his circumcised penis. So Rafiq took his shorts off carefully, keeping his penis covered. After all, he was still Ram Parshad.

There was an announcement on the station's loud speaker: "Attention! Attention! Soon a train is going to pass through this station. It is carrying Muslim refugees to Pakistan and is guarded by soldiers of the Muslim Baloch Regiment. These soldiers often shoot Sikhs if they see them. All Sikhs therefore should take cover." This announcement was repeated two or three times. The train came; it passed very slowly along the platform 1. It was packed with people, both inside and on the roof. It did not stop. How we wished it had stopped and taken us to Pakistan!²

It rained heavily during the night but the tin roof over the platform kept us dry. Dharam told us what had happened at Uchi Bassi when that young Muslim was dragged back into the train. "I was in the carriage into which the Sikh policeman dragged the man back. A few minutes later after the train left Uchi Bassi, the policeman raised his rifle and aimed at the Muslim while shouting obscenities. The Muslim begged to be spared. I too entreated the policeman to let him go, but the policeman pulled the trigger. The Muslim slumped on the floor. He was still breathing when the policeman thrust his bayonet into his chest and dragged his body and threw it out of the train." Now we knew what that sound was which we had heard.

In a few hours light started to appear in the sky. We had to decide what to do. Dharam offered to take us to the nearest temple. "There is usually a place near the temple for poor Hindus to stay. You can stay there. I can get the appropriate symbols for you so that you are not challenged again." He meant things like a thread around the neck and a *tikka* or *bindi* on the forehead. He was a kind man and wanted to do all he could to keep us alive.

My mother demurred. To go to a temple seemed to her a long shot. After all, we should now be able to catch a direct train from Jalandhar to Lahore, she thought. "Can we not wait for the train here?" she asked.

"I doubt there is any regular service from Jalandhar to Lahore anymore," Dharam said. "In any case, after what happened at Khudda Kurala, it would be suicidal to take another train." When Dharam was in the stationmaster's room getting Rafiq bandaged, he heard that a small contingent of army troops was stationed at the station. He now offered to go and look for them; they might be able to help us.

While he was gone, two Sikhs walked up to us.

"Who are you?" one of them asked.

"We are Hindus waiting for the next train to Amritsar," answered my mother. Amritsar was in India; she could not possibly say we were waiting for the train to Lahore.

"How do we know you are not Muslims?" he asked. "Come with me to the waiting room," he said to Rafiq. He obviously wanted to check his penis. When Rafiq did not move, the Sikh started to pull him by his arm. My mother caught Rafiq's other arm to stop him being dragged by the Sikh. Exactly at that moment Dharam returned with a uniformed soldier. Seeing the soldier, the two Sikhs slunk away. Dharam had told the soldier the truth; that we were Muslims and needed protection. The soldier was part of a Madrasi Regiment and, being a Southern Indian, had no particular sympathy for either the Muslims or the Sikhs in Punjab. He took us to the Female Waiting Room which was next to the room where Madrasi soldiers were staying. Dharam now said goodbye to us. He had saved our lives. We never saw him again.

The Madrasi soldiers were kind and showed genuine sympathy when Majida tearfully told our story in English, the only language in which they could communicate with us. "There is no Muslim refugee camp near here," they said. "But we will try to send you to a Muslim *muhalla* which is currently under military guard. There, resident Muslims are taking Muslim refugees into their homes. As for Rafiq, we will see if we can get him admitted to the military hospital in Jalandhar Cantonment."

Later in the morning a soldier came to our room. "We have a truck outside the station. The driver will take you to the Muslim *muhalla*." The truck was actually delivering food to the soldiers but the driver had kindly agreed to take us to the Muslim *muhalla*

I remember walking out of the dark waiting room into the hot Indian summer sun and being suddenly overwhelmed by a sense of terror and utter unreality. Passing shadows leapt out at me, sending me cowering. A distant sound was like a clash of swords. I felt like someone who wakes up and finds that all that was familiar had vanished. Did I know then that however long I lived, how many years might come and go, I would always be hostage to the memory of what had come to pass on that train?

The truck driver first stopped at the military hospital, where we dropped Rafiq off. Then we went to the Muslim *muhalla*, where a Muslim, Aslam Khan, took us to his home. He had a wife and two boys. They treated us as part of their family and we stayed with them for about one week. One day during the week, while we were playing on the roof, I heard Majida calling from downstairs: *"Abaji* is here!" *"Abaji* is here!" I rushed down. My father was there with Major Bhagwan Das. My father grabbed me and kissed me. I was crying. Major Bhagwan Das put his hand on my head as Indians do when they want to console someone. We talked quickly as they were in a hurry. My father said he was determined to find out what had happened to Rashida. He gave some money to my mother, and then he and Major Bhagwan Das left.

Aslam Khan's family was well-connected and was able to find space in a truck with an armed guard to take us all to Pakistan. The truck was packed with Muslim refugees. I remember when we crossed the border into Pakistan, the people shouted *"Pakistan zindabad"* and embraced each other.

In Lahore we were dropped at the Walton Refugee Camp, which was the largest refugee camp in Lahore. It had hundreds of volunteers who brought *dal* and *rotis* to feed us. We only stayed one or two days in the camp. My mother had the address where Uncle Jamil was staying. It was in a street off Anarkali, near Qutubuddin Aibak's tomb. I do not have to tell you how Uncle Jamil reacted when my mother told him that his and his brothers' families had been destroyed!

4

Rafiq writes: *I was admitted to the military hospital in Jalandhar. I was in a large ward and all the patients were Muslims who had been injured in the communal violence. The bullet in my left thigh* was successfully removed the same evening. (The doctor gave me the brass fragments of the bullet and I kept them for many years but I have lost them). There was no Muslim staff left in the hospital. The food was virtually nonexistent. Only a handful of rice was given us each day. One morning, an English military officer, I think he was a brigadier or something, visited the hospital. As I was the only patient who was able to speak a little English, I told him of the terrible food. He asked that more food be given to the patients. That day we were given two rations of rice, but it was back to one the following day. My dressing was changed every day but otherwise there was no nursing. As you know, in India it is the family who comes and nurses the patients in the hospital, and the patients in that ward had no family members. Some patients just defecated in their beds. My problem, on the other hand, was severe constipation. On a small portion of rice, my bowels refused to move. Day after day, I begged for a laxative, but was refused. The third or fourth time I asked for a laxative, the person in charge of the ward said to me, "If you keep bothering us we will send you out of the hospital and the Sikhs will give you a proper laxative." Need I tell you what he meant?

One day a Muslim was admitted with a broken leg which was amputated in the hospital. He was a tonga driver. The Sikhs had waylaid him, broken his leg, and taken off with his tonga. He was delirious the whole night and loudly kept reciting the kalma. In the morning he called me to his bed and said, "Can you please check if my leg is still there?" I knew it had been amputated, but I did not have the heart to tell him. So I lied to him and said, "Yes, it is still there." He thanked me and repeated the kalma.

It was the third or fourth day after my admission that Father, with Major Bhagwan Das, came to visit me in the hospital. I was thrilled to see them. I wrapped my arms around abaji and started crying. Abaji was crying too. He told me that he had just been to visit you in the Muslim muhalla and that you were all right. He said that he was making enquiries about sister Rashida. He gave me five rupees. He was only there for a few minutes because Major Bhagwan Das had to leave. I now wish he had taken me with him back to Mukerian. Better still, if he had come to see me first he could then have taken *me and united me with you in the Muslim* muhalla. *These are just afterthoughts, you know.*

I had been hearing stories from the staff and the patients of the terrible things happening outside the hospital. They told me that the law had completely broken down and the Sikhs constantly prowled the area. "They look out for the patients who are discharged from the hospital and assassinate them, there and then," they said. One day, three patients were discharged. A few hours later, one returned and told us that the other two were caught and murdered. I was really scared, as the person in charge of the ward was now talking of discharging me.[3]

The constipation was unrelenting. I was worried that I was going to die unless relieved. I imagined the contents in my intestine hardening to stone. "How can a man survive without a bowel movement?" I thought. As you know, we Indians are rather obsessed with our bowels!

At the same time I was constantly thinking of reaching Pakistan. Walking out of the hospital was suicidal. There were two possibilities. One was to reach the protected Muslim muhalla where you people were staying; the other was to find an escorted convoy to Pakistan. The Muslim muhalla was ten miles from the hospital and, as I said, those ten miles were death traps. I asked the hospital authorities if they could give me some protection under which I could reach the muhalla *but they flatly refused. And where else could I find a secure transportation?*

One day I heard that some trucks were coming to the hospital to pick up wounded patients from this hospital and take them to Pakistan. Three trucks came in the evening. They parked in the hospital driveway. I went out to investigate but one of the hospital orderlies saw me and ordered me back to the ward. However, I slipped out again. A number of wounded were lying on the floor of the trucks. I approached one of the soldiers who appeared to be in charge of the trucks. He was a Pathan and heard me sympathetically. He said he personally would have no objection to taking me but the hospital was going to decide who would go. He said they could only take the more serious ones. There were so many more serious than me, and the space in the trucks was so limited, that I lost hope. What could I do?

I went back to my bed and waited till all were asleep. I then sneaked out and climbed into one truck which was empty, and sat down in one corner, trying to hide myself. I sat there till the daybreak, when one of the hospital orderlies found me and told me in most severe terms that I would be expelled from the hospital and handed over to the Sikhs if I tried to play such games again. Utterly despondent, I returned to my bed but did not give up. I realized it was now or never. I was afraid to be absent from the bed because the dressing man came early in the morning. He would notice my absence and report it. So I said to the patient in the next bed, "If the dressing man comes, tell him that I had to go to the bathroom, that I was very constipated, and probably would be squatting in the lavatory for long time." Then I slipped out again. This time I immediately ran into that Pathan officer and begged him to take me. He ordered me to jump in the truck as the wounded patients were being loaded.

The rest of the journey went smoothly. It did not take long for us to reach Lahore. I remember the tremendous sense of relief as we crossed the border. Even the wounded shouted "Pakistan zindabad." On the way to the border I had seen trucks going in the opposite direction filled with Hindus and Sikhs. They were shouting "Jai Hind." I also saw at least one kafla *of Muslims walking towards the border. The* kafla *was guarded by a few Muslim soldiers. There must have been thousands and thousands of people. Interspersed amongst the people were some* gadas *pulled by bullocks; the infirm and dying were lying on them. "Where do they get their food from?" I wondered, "and water, for that matter?" They were travelling in a country which had suddenly become their graveyard. I was so lucky to be in a truck.*

I was dropped at the Mayo Hospital in Lahore. I remember the hospital was overflowing with wounded refugees. They changed my dressing but there was no question of being admitted. I was put in a truck along with others and sent to the Walton Refugee Camp. Unfortunately, I did not know the address of Uncle Jamil, and I did not know anyone else in Lahore. I remained at the camp for two or three days and then went in a truck to the Lahore Railway Station. I was planning to take the train to Lyallpur and meet up there with brother Bashir. I was told that the train to Lyallpur would not leave for another two or three days. Fortunately, I met a young man at the station who took pity on me and took me to his house which was not far from the station and where I stayed two or three nights. Finally, I caught the train to Lyallpur but could only find the space on the roof of the train. I can tell you that I had to fight hard to find a space on the roof. As the train left Lahore station, I remember seeing a few Sikh corpses lying beside the train tracks, with vultures feasting on them. It took about twelve hours for the train to reach Lyallpur. It rained almost all the time while I was sitting on the roof.

And so it all ended, in recrimination and bloodshed. Sixty years on, those who witnessed this catastrophe are fast disappearing, and the catastrophe itself is becoming a footnote in history. But for those of us who witnessed its horror and are still alive, it will ever be the heart of darkness, its memory a burden we must carry to our graves. It was a mammoth human sacrifice to the gods of Indian independence. Was it worth it?

5

My father, who died in 1974, told us: *I heard of the train massacre the following day, on August 24, when the train arrived back in Mukerian from Jalandhar. It was early afternoon and I was in the hospital seeing patients. I dropped everything and hurried to the railway station. The train was still on the platform. I went into the stationmaster's room. The stationmaster called the train driver. He was the same driver who had driven the train the day before. He was a short dark Hindu. He confirmed that a massacre of Muslims had occurred at Khudda Kurala station the day before. He had no part in it, he said, and he knew nothing about it in advance. He was forced by the armed Sikhs to keep the train at the station while they did the killings. I believe the driver was innocent, though he did not seem to be too upset about the massacre. The stationmaster, however, was distressed and commiserated with me. "Things are really getting very bad, Doctor Sahib," he said.*

I asked the driver, "Do you think anybody escaped the massacre?"

"It was pretty thorough," he said, "There were hundreds of armed Sikhs. A number of passengers reached Jalandhar Station. Most of them of course were Hindus and Sikhs but if any Muslims escaped they would have been amongst them. I know Jalandhar station has an army unit to protect people."

I returned home and told Hamida what I had heard. We were totally stunned and devastated. Hamida put her arms around me and started crying. I was crying too. It was getting dark then, and there was not much I could do. We spent the night mostly awake and kept talking to each other. As you know, Hamida was the most religious in our family and had a strong belief in God, Heaven and Hell. "I am sure they have been martyred and gone to heaven," she kept saying. I was so glad she had her faith to fall back on; it provided at least some solace she so desperately needed. I was just too numb to feel anything.

The following morning I bicycled to Major Bhagwan Das's bivouac. Fortunately, he was there. He was very sympathetic. I asked him if he would take me immediately to Khudda Kurala. He did not think there was much point in going to Khudda Kurala. "The Sikhs would have returned to their villages and be impossible to trace," he said. "It is better to go to Jalandhar station. If any Muslims escaped, the military there would know." He offered to take me to Jalandhar.

The following day Major Bhagwan Das picked me up at the hospital in his truck with two armed soldiers. I was afraid to leave Hamida alone, so I took her to Ramzan's house. Bhagwan Das and I drove to the Jalandhar station and met the Madrasi soldiers. They told me that some of my family had indeed survived the massacre. They knew about me as Majida had told them that her father was the Medical Officer at Mukerian. They gave us the address of the Muslim muhalla.. There, at the house where refugees were being received and processed, we were told that my family was at Aslam Khan's house. That is how we found you. Afterwards I went to see Rafiq at the military hospital, and then Major Bhagwan Das and I returned to Mukerian.

Hamida was so happy to hear that most of our family was safe, though the disappearance of Rashida and the destruction of our relatives and friends were devastating. I now tried to find out what *had happened to Rashida. I contacted two persons for help: Bansi Lal and Joginder Singh. Bansi Lal agreed to go to Khudda Kurala by train the following day. There, he talked to a number of people and was told that of all the girls kidnapped from the train, only the young and uneducated were kept alive, the older ones were slaughtered the same day. The Sikhs were afraid of the older girls; they were worried that they would have the know-how to contact the authorities, or at least would try to run away. Rashida, being a university graduate, had no chance. On the way back from Khudda Kurala, Bansi Lal stopped at Dasuya and went to the police station. Khudda Kurala was in the jurisdiction of Dasuya police station. At the police station Bansi Lal was told that the police had already investigated the massacre and had reliable information that all older or literate girls had been killed.*

Joginder Singh came to see me too. He said how sorry he was, and that the massacre was a complete surprise to him. He too offered to go to Khudda Kurala. After a couple of days he came again and said the he had been to Khudda Kurala. He said he had in fact asked the Sikhs to dig up the mass grave where Muslim victims were buried and had recognized the body of Rashida. He even told me the colour of the shalwar-kameez she was wearing. Hamida, who remembered Rashidas's dress when she left home, said that it was not the right colour. Rashida obviously would not have changed clothes between the kidnapping and the assassination. In any case, how did Joginder Singh recognize Rashida? He had never seen her.

Things were now really dangerous in Mukerian so I decided to send Hamida to Mirpur. I thought Mirpur will be safer than Mukerian. Even in the hospital the tension was growing. The Hindu servants were now becoming hostile and refusing to carry out my orders. Only Bansi Lal stood by me throughout. One day a Muslim family came to see me. They had a relative in the military who had brought an armed truck to take them to Pakistan. They had extra space and offered to take me with them. I thought the time had come for me to leave, and so I locked the house, gave one key to Bansi Lal, and left. Even then it never occurred to me that it was final. I still thought that things would get back to normal and we would return.

As you know, Rashida's husband, Captain Khursheed, made a final attempt to trace her a few weeks later. He was in the military and was able to take a military truck to Khudda Kurala. He roamed the villages for a number of days but could not find her. We have no doubt that she was killed. Captain Khursheed, however, was successful in contacting Hamida in Mirpur and brought her to Pakistan.

I still don't know what to think of Joginder Singh. We were such close friends. I looked after his family like my own. Did he deceive me? Did he know all along that we were going to be massacred and did not tell me? He was the top Akali leader in the area. Was it possible for Akalis to plan a massacre on this scale, involving hundreds of Sikhs, without his knowledge? Was he even the real planner of the massacre? Did his commitment to his co-religionists overcome his loyalty to a close friend? Was his account of digging the mass grave and seeing Rashida a cock-and-bull story?

Late at night, I often think of the people who played their roles in that cataclysmic tragedy which overtook our family on August 23. I think of Joginder Singh and that he might have betrayed me. But then I immediately think of Bansi Lal, Major Bhagwan Das, and above all, Dharam Pal. You see, I have to do that; otherwise how can I keep faith in humanity?

EPILOGUE

One Muslim is equal to ten infidels. Remember Badr.
The Drill Master

1

After spending a few days in Lahore, it was time for my father to look for a job. He was penniless and we had nothing but the clothes we had on. So he went to the Provincial Ministry of Health in Lahore. Fortunately, he had no difficulty in finding a position with the government; numerous hospitals were without doctors. In Punjab there were more Hindu and Sikh doctors than Muslims, so with the transfer of population there were many more vacancies in West (Pakistani) Punjab than in the East. My father could choose almost anywhere he wanted to work. He chose a small town, Toba Tek Singh, about 120 miles southwest of Lahore. My father always preferred to work in small towns where he was often the only government doctor. Perhaps he wanted to be his own boss. Also, we had some friends near Toba Tek Singh.

Toba Tek Singh in those days was a quiet small town of about 5000 people. Soon after, it became famous because of a short story written by the famous Urdu writer Sadat Hassan Monto. The story, which has assumed almost a cult following and has been made into a movie, is set in the Lahore Mental Hospital immediately after Independence. The transfer of population between two halves of Punjab has just been completed. Hindus and Sikhs have gone to the Indian Punjab and the Muslims to the Pakistani Punjab, but what to do with the inmates of the Lahore Mental Hospital, who are still a mixture of Hindus, Muslims and Sikhs? Lahore is now in Pakistan and the Hindu and Sikh patients have to be taken to India. One of the inmates calls himself Toba Tek Singh. He claims he is from Toba Tek Singh and only wants to go back to Toba Tek Singh. But he can't because Toba Tek

Singh is in Pakistan and no Sikh can live there. Toba Tek Singh is therefore put in a truck, along with the other Hindu and Sikh inmates of the hospital, and taken to the border. But Toba Tek Singh refuses to go any further and lies down on the border. The story, written in a dark and despairing mood, suggests that in a country gone mad, Toba Tek Singh and other patients of the mental hospital are the only sane people left.

So our family took the train to Toba Tek Singh. The small hospital there was located in a relatively large and pleasant compound with trees and bushes. The doctor's house, made of mud, was fairly primitive, though spacious. Sikhs had been a prominent community in Toba Tek Singh and the surrounding villages, but by now they had either been murdered or left. There were still some Hindus in town, though they had been relocated to the centre of the town for their own security and were waiting repatriation to India under armed guard. The local SDO (Sub-divisional Officer) invited my father to a storeroom and gave him a few clothes, blankets, and utensils, which the police had collected from the abandoned Hindu and Sikh homes. It felt strange to be sleeping under sheets whose owners might have been murdered in their own homes, and to be wearing a sweater, for it was winter by now, whose rightful owner had probably been hacked to pieces. It was almost a year before my father had enough money to buy a clock; till then we could only guess the time of the day, like primitive people, from the movements of the sun.

Soon after arriving, my father took me to the local school called District Board High School. The school had classes from grade 6 to grade 10. In Mukerian I had been in grade 7 and I was expected to be admitted to the same grade, but we had no records of any kind to show. The headmaster arranged for two masters to test me to see if I had knowledge expected of a grade 7 student. I passed the tests and was taken to be introduced to the students of grade 7.

So started my life at the District Board High School, Toba Tek Singh. I was to attend that school till I matriculated at the end of grade 10.

2

The school was a brick building with dirt grounds and few trees. Most of the teachers, like the doctors, had been Hindus and Sikhs and had departed. The few teachers left had to do multiple tasks, like teaching subjects of which they knew little. We rarely had a full day of classes. Sometimes we sat in the class talking for hours because there was no teacher. There were days when the headmaster had to send all the students home immediately after the morning assembly as no teacher showed up.

After the first year, my parents began to worry about the poor education I was receiving at the school. There was of course no parent-teacher association to do anything about it. Most students came from surrounding villages and their parents were, more often than not, illiterate. The district board, which ran the school, was as dysfunctional as any other institution in Pakistan in those days. So my father decided that the only way for me to make any progress was to get extra tutoring at home. Fortunately he found a tutor, Master Suleiman, who was a qualified teacher but had gone to Lahore and taken a law degree. He had returned to Toba Tek Singh hoping to build his law practice but it was not easy. Though there was no shortage of cases for a lawyer, considering all the property and land disputes, people had little money. So Master Suleiman was glad to make a little extra money from private tuition.

There was, however, the small problem of finding a suitable place to meet for my tutorials. Master Suleiman could only come in the evening after finishing his work in the courthouse. We could not sit outside as it was dark by then and cold too in the winter months. An indoor place had to be found. Our house had only two rooms and both were full of *charpoys* and there was no place for a table and two chairs. In any case Master Suleiman could not enter the house and use any room without my mother and sisters retreating in the other room because of *purdah*. So it was decided that the only place available for the tutorial was the cowshed behind the house. It was really a buffalo shed rather than a cowshed. My father had by now bought a buffalo to provide unadulterated milk for the family as the milk bought from the shop was always diluted with water. We were used to having house buffaloes; they were easy to buy and sell. My father had an almost mystical belief in the nutritive value of pure milk especially buffalo's milk with its high fat content.

Anyway, the buffalo was moved to one side of the shed and we were able to find a little space to squeeze a small table and two simple chairs. A hurricane lamp on the table provided the light. Sitting for an hour in the shed was not easy, with flies buzzing and moths attracted by the light of the lantern, not to mention the overpowering smell of the buffalo's excrements. I was embarrassed that we could not provide a better place for these tutorials, but otherwise all went well. Master Suleiman was an excellent teacher and helped me for the rest of my time in school.

3

The two most important subjects in school were math and English. English was never a problem; my father could help me with it, and we often used English at home anyway. My father had again started subscribing to the daily The Civil and Military Gazette, as he had done before 1947, though the newspaper had fallen on hard times and closed down soon afterwards.

The headmaster, with the Kiplingesque name of Sher Khan, took our English class. He was a short slim man with a trim greying beard and wore a round cap. He was provided with a house in the school compound and as the school was adjacent to the hospital, the headmaster and my family were on friendly terms. The headmaster was very fond of English grammar and usually started the class by asking a grammar question. He would write a sentence on the board like: "Asif said to Hamid, 'As it is a nice evening, we should go for a walk'." He would then call on one of the students to come forward and write the sentence in an indirect clause: "Asif said to Hamid that as it was a nice evening they should go for a walk." He was so fond of these direct/indirect clauses that we called him "Master direct/indirect."

The English books we used in the school had not yet been revised and had been put together many years before Independence by British teachers working in India. They were a delightful compilation of short stories and poems and included excerpts from well-known novels and dramas. All the great English writers were represented. I remember when the headmaster introduced us to Shakespeare with the poem from 'The Tempest', "Full fathom five thy father lies." At the start of the class he asked how many of us had heard of Shakespeare. A few of us raised our hands. He pointed to me. I stood up and said, "He was a famous writer, sir." "I don't think you quite understand," said the headmaster. "Shakespeare was far more than a famous writer. He was the greatest writer who ever lived. Let me tell you that the English people revere him the way we revere our prophet Muhammad (peace be on him)." I had never heard of Shakespeare compared to our Prophet, but the headmaster's point was no doubt driven home.

I had little to do in the long summer holidays except to read. Other students had responsibilities to help their family by feeding the cattle or plowing the fields, but I had none. Sitting outside under the huge *bohr* tree, surrounded by its numerous prop roots, I read whatever I could find, mostly books of English fiction bought by my father from a secondhand bookstore in Lyallpur where he often went as medico-legal witness. Filling those interminable summer days is what started my love of the English language. In one book of short stories there was a story called "Rab and His Friends." It was a true story written by a medical student in Edinburgh about a woman with breast cancer, her husband, and their dog, Rab. The woman stoically underwent surgery — this was before chloroform was discovered. However, she died postoperatively with sepsis. Her husband, too, died soon afterwards. Rab was heartbroken and could live no longer; he refused to eat or drink, and died. I read the story again and again and was deeply moved by it. It remained with me for the rest of my life. In later life I wanted to read the story again but could not find it. Whenever I met a doctor from Edinburgh I asked, "Do you know a story called 'Rab and His Friends'?" Nobody I met had heard of it. Years later, now with a computer at hand, I Googled the story's name and was delighted not only to download the story but to find all kinds of information about the author, Dr. John Brown, who wrote it in 1859. It was quite an emotional experience for me to read the story more than fifty years later.

One day my father brought home a copy of 'Wuthering Heights'. It was a soft-cover edition with a painting of a man carrying a woman in his arms on the cover, and underneath it said: 'The greatest love story ever told'. I don't know how many times I read 'Wuthering Heights' that summer. Tears would well in my eyes when I reached the end where Heathcliff is buried "to the scandal of the whole neighborhood." By the end of the summer I could recite pages of the book from my memory. "You are a *hafiz*" my mother would say teasingly, "though not of Quran." My mother was a very perceptive person and noticed my daydreaming. "You are the most sensitive of my children," she would say, "and I love you for that, but sometimes I do worry about you." I was the youngest in the family and my aging parents felt that they might die before I was able to take care of myself. It was a harsh world out there.

4

Each class in our school had a 'sports period' supervised by the 'drill master'. Usually we drilled during this period, though occasionally we played soccer. The drill master was a tall man with a trimmed moustache. I cannot recall his name but he was always dressed in a khaki *shalwar- kameez*, appropriate for a drill master. He decided to give a special name to each of the five classes he supervised. He selected names from Islamic history, like the names of early Caliphs, or of famous battles. This was his innovation, his way of acknowledging the new Muslim state we now lived in. My class was called the Badr Class. We all knew a little about the Battle of Badr; without Badr there would be no Muslims in this world. The drill master loved to tell us the story of Badr. Prophet Muhammad had been driven out of Mecca and taken refuge in Medina. Meccans sent a big force to capture him. Muhammad, with his pathetically small and ill-equipped group of followers, came out of Medina to face the Meccans. The battle was fought on the grounds of Badr. The Muslims fought with ferocity hitherto unknown to the world. After all, had not their prophet told them on the eve of the battle that before a drop of martyr's blood touched the ground, the martyr was received by *houris* in paradise? Meccans retreated against this ferocious attack. After Badr, Islam never looked back and within a few years brought the great empires of the time to their knees. "So you should be proud that I am calling you the Badr Class," the drill master said. Occasionally, the drill master would start talking about India and how the British should have handed the whole country to the Muslims. "After all, we were the rulers before the British," he said. He was certain that we could still defeat India. "Each Muslim is equal to ten *kafirs*," he declared. "Remember Badr!" he said to prove his point.[1]

Our drill master also decided that we should learn to drill with rifles. After all, in his mind we were the young fighters he was training to re-conquer India and establish a new Muslim empire. He persuaded the school to get wooden replicas of the rifles which a local carpenter made out of cheap wood. We must have looked quite ridiculous strutting back and forth with these 'rifles' on the dusty school ground, pretending to be the formative nucleus of a great Muslim army, but the drill master was very proud that he was successful in introducing this new martial feature in our sporting activities.

5

The standard of learning in our school was further eroded by hasty efforts to modify our curriculum to the new reality of Pakistan. This was particularly true of the history books which were completely revised. The early Hindu period of Indian history was abbreviated, the British period made to look incidental, and the Muslim period was greatly expanded. Leaving aside the contents, the books were badly printed and poorly bound. The first thing we did after buying the books from the small local bookstore was to take them to the school *chaprasi* who, to make a little extra money, rebound them.

According to the new history book, the age of enlightenment in India started with the Muslim (Arab) invasion of India. The book introduced the two iconic figures of Indian Muslim history: Muhammad bin Qasim and Mahmud of Ghazni. Before these two warriors, India, we were told, was a land of superstition and a million gods. Truth, I leant later, was not that simple.

India's first contact with the Muslims was a land-sea military expedition ordered by Hajjaj bin Yousef, the governor of Jeddah, and sanctioned by Caliph Abdul Malik[2] to punish Sindhi pirates, based in the area of the present-day Karachi, who were successfully preying on Muslim shipping boats doing business between the Arab lands and South India. The precipitating event was the abduction by the pirates of some Muslim women coming for the Hajj from Serendip.[3]

The Arab expedition was led by the legendry Muhammad bin Qasim, Hajjaj's nephew and son-in-law, who was only eighteen at the time. Arriving in Sind in 711CE, Qasim occupied a number of cities, defeated King Dahar, whose head he sent as a souvenir to Hajjaj[4] and, in the custom of the day, dealt harshly with the vanquished infidels (who, incidentally, were Buddhists, not Hindus). Qasim had plans to continue his advance into India but both Caliph Abdul Malik and Hajjaj had died, and Qasim was recalled from India by the new Caliph Walid and executed. The execution of this iconic general has been much bemoaned by the Muslims. They believe that had Qasim lived and allowed to continue his invasion of India, he would have been unstoppable. The details of Qasim's execution are murky. The traditional Muslim historians ascribe it to the new Caliph's fear and jealousy of the young Qasim. A lengthy history of Sind called *Chach Nama*[5] gives different account of Qasim's death. According to *Chach Nama*, Qasim sent two daughters of King Dahar as presents to the new Caliph in Baghdad for his harem. When the Caliph found out that the girls were not virgins and in fact had already been forced to submit to Qasim, he was furious and ordered that Qasim be sewn in camel's hide and returned to Damascus. When Qasim expired en route to Damascus, the girls admitted to the Caliph that they made up their story to take revenge on Qasim for their father's death. The Caliph immediately ordered that the two girls be buried alive in a wall.[6]

Muhammad bin Qasim's invasion of India was not unprovoked. He was carrying out orders to punish Raja Dahar for acts of piracy in the Indian Ocean, though it is unlikely that Raja Dahar had any control on the pirates. The next great Muslim conqueror of India invaded India not to punish but to plunder. Mahmud of Ghazni was a remarkable warrior whose father rose from obscurity in Afghanistan to carve out a small kingdom. Mahmud learned his fighting skills well, and India was an easy target. Indians, always relying on elephants, could never match the fast and nimble Afghan cavalry. Mahmud knew that the riches of India were mostly stored in its vast temples. He made seventeen forays into Western India, almost a yearly ritual at the end of the monsoon season, and every time he targeted a new temple. He was not an indiscriminate killer, nor was he particularly interested in the spread of Islam, though to the idols in the Hindu temples he showed no mercy. "I am *butshikan*, not a *butprust*," he shouted as he smashed the idols. Prophet Muhammad had denounced idolatry in such strong terms that idol worship had become an anathema to Muslims, and idol destruction an article of faith. Mahmud's last invasion, in which he raided the famous temple of Somnath, was the most daring and no doubt most despairing to the Hindus. To the Muslims, on the other hand, it was the epic of Muslim triumph. Somnath, situated on the western coast of Gujarat, was one of the richest temples in India and housed a revered idol. According to one historian, the temple had an endowment of more than 10,000 villages, and a thousand Brahmans and five hundred female dancers were employed in worshipping its *lingam*. Fanciful stories have grown around Somnath invasion. According to one, the temple's central idol hung in the air unsupported. When Mahmud saw it, he could not believe it. He was then told that the idol was made of metal and was hanging in the air because of magnets in the ceiling. Another story relates how, when the idol was smashed, vast quantities of precious jewels and gold spilled forth from the its belly. Yet another story tells Mahmud carrying the huge gates of the temple to Ghazni as souvenir. A further story tells us that Somnath was a corruption of Menat, the idol in Mecca which Prophet Muhammad was supposed to have destroyed but was in fact secretly taken to Gujarat where it was ensconced in the temple.[7]

    The last chapter in the history book was devoted to the Indian Independence Movement and was a screed against Gandhi, Nehru, Mountbatten, and Radcliffe. The last two, we learned from our new history book, had played directly into the Hindu hands. Mountbatten was cuckolded by Nehru, and Radcliffe, who was responsible for drawing the boundary between the two countries, was heavily bribed by rich Indian merchants. Though more scholarly books have questioned Mountbatten's integrity, the criticism of Radcliffe was completely unjustified. It was simply impossible for him to partition the country to the satisfaction of all. Radcliffe's dilemma has been well summed up by W.H. Auden:

> *Unbiased at least he was when he arrived on his mission,*
> *Having never set eyes on the land he was called to partition*
> *Between two peoples fanatically at odds,*
> *With their different diets and incompatible gods.*
> *"Time," they had briefed him in London, "is short. It's too late*
> *For mutual reconciliation or rational debate;*
> *The only solution now lies in separation.*
> *The Viceroy thinks, as you will see from his letter,*
> *That the less you are seen in his company the better,*
> *So we've arranged to provide you with other accommodation.*
> *We can give you four judges, two Moslem and two Hindu,*
> *To consult with, but the final decision must rest with you."*
>
> *Shut up in a lonely mansion, with police night and day*
> *Patrolling the gardens to keep the assassins away,*
> *He got down to work, to the task of settling the fate*
> *Of millions. The maps at his disposal were out of date*
> *And the Census Returns almost certainly incorrect.*
> *But there was no time to check them, no time to inspect*
> *Contested areas. The weather was frightfully hot,*
> *And a bout of dysentery kept him constantly on the trot,*
> *But in seven weeks it was done, the frontiers decided,*
> *A continent for better or worse divided.*
>
> *The next day he sailed for England, where he could quickly forget*
> *The case, as a good lawyer must. Return he would not,*
> *Afraid, as he told his Club, that he might get shot.*

6

Soon after arriving in Toba Tek Singh, Majida found a job at the local Government Girls' High School. Every morning she walked to work wearing a *burqa*. Though many poor women went about in public without *burqa*, it was not considered appropriate for middle-class women to go out barefaced. The teachers in the Girls' School, as in my school, did not have regular parent-teacher meetings but it was not uncommon to summon a parent to school if a student was creating problems. In the Girls' School it was almost always the mother who came, but if the mother or any other close female relative was not available, the father was allowed to come to the school. It had always been up to the teacher to meet with the father either face to face, or to talk to him from behind a curtain or a wall. This had been an acceptable practice and the young headmistress of the school saw no problem with it.

It did not take long for the gossip that some teachers at the Girls' School had interviewed fathers without *purdah* to reach the *maulvi* at the mosque. Maulvi Tamizuddin was not a fundamentalist as we think of them these days, and he probably would not have condoned stoning for adultery or amputation for stealing. Nevertheless, in the new Islamic country he regarded himself as a guardian of morals. He was a severe diabetic and a patient of my father. As he knew that my sister taught at the school, he thought it prudent to come and see my father, before raising the issue during the Friday sermon at the mosque.

"Doctor Sahib, I hear that the headmistress is allowing teachers to talk to the fathers without *purdah*. You know, this is not in accordance with our religion."

"But Maulvi Sahib, I think this has been accepted in the schools all along."

"That is exactly the point, Doctor Sahib. We are independent now. With God's grace, we are free to make our own policies. We are not living under British rule or Hindu *samraj*."

"You know, Maulvi Sahib, that my daughter observes *purdah* in public. She wears a *burqa* to school. The headmistress does not force teachers to talk to the fathers without *purdah*. It is an option."

"We hear that the young headmistress is very strong-headed. Out of respect for you, I am not going to do anything for the time being. I would like you to talk to the headmistress through your daughter. I am sure this is something we can solve peacefully."

Maulvi Tamizuddin left, leaving his implicit warning. My father talked to Majida the same evening, who took the message to the headmistress. The headmistress pooh-poohed the whole thing. "These *mullahs*," she said, "they live in a Neanderthal world. I do not have to listen to them."

But my father knew better. If Maulvi Tamizuddin made a public announcement during Friday sermon, there might not be many people bold enough to come to the headmistress's defense.

My father wanted to settle the issue outside the mosque. The headmistress was a very dedicated teacher, and such teachers were few and far between.

My father decided to invite Maulvi Tamizuddin for another meeting to which my father also invited a friend, Hajji Wajid Husain, a prominent and well-respected local businessman who had lived in Toba Tek Singh for a long time and had been very generous to my father when my father arrived penniless in 1947. My father's idea was that Hajji Sahib might be able to persuade Maulvi Sahib to drop the matter. It was a cordial meeting. Hajji Sahib tried to convince Maulvi Sahib that *purdah* in Islam was not obligatory, but optional. This led to a prolonged discussion. Wajid Husain was an intelligent man who could quote passages from Quran and *Hadith* to show that prophet's wives themselves had gone barefaced and in fact had participated in battles ministering to the wounded Muslim fighters. The problem with Quran and *Hadith* is that you can often find passages and stories in them to support contrary positions. It was Hajji Sahib's advice, therefore, that the headmistress would be wise to enforce *purdah*. "It is a small issue," he said, "and we don't want the Maulvi Sahib to bring it out in public." My father invited the headmistress to our house and told her what had happened. The headmistress, however strong willed, was after all a woman in an increasingly Muslim country. She acquiesced.

It was also about this time that a touring cinema company we called "talkie," came to town and pitched its tent in a large open space. Touring talkies were an old custom in small towns where there were no permanent movie houses. As the talkie was a great success, the owner decided that in a growing city like Toba Tek Singh it might be profitable to build a permanent cinema house. Consequently, he applied to the city for permission to build one and the permission was granted. When the news reached Maulvi Tamizuddin, he reacted against it. He had tolerated a temporary talkie with some reluctance, he thundered, but this permanent cinema, potentially a perpetual den of inequity, was going too far. Maulvi Sahib then declared that he would call upon the youth of the city to demolish the building as soon as it was built. The businessman who had submitted the proposal had no appetite for confrontation. He withdrew the application.

7

In the morning we always had the school assembly on the school ground before we walked to our respective classrooms. During the assembly we stood in long rows, each grade forming its own line and sang songs in Urdu, led by a student with a loud voice. Early on, they were songs asking the God to enable us to be better students, to be obedient to our teachers and parents, and to lead a clean life, free from selfishness and greed. Soon, the songs were replaced by recitation from Quran. It was in Arabic, of course, and nobody understood its meaning. One student who was *hafiz-e-Quran* did the recitation. At the end of the prayer we all said "amen."

One morning, when I was in grade 9, as I walked to the school ground for the assembly, I saw not only the students and teachers but also three or four policemen in uniform. Instead of the usual shouting and jostling, the students, seeing the police, were quiet and apprehensive. The assembly was opened as usual by recitation from the Quran but instead of the headmaster, the chief of police, the *thanidar*, stepped in front of the assembly. He was brief and to the point: "Last night," he said, "someone entered the school compound and scrawled outside the classroom walls, nefarious slogans against the headmaster. The police are taking it very seriously. Whoever has done it will be severely punished. If any of you has been instigated by someone outside the school to write these slogans, I warn you not to do it again. Such things will not be tolerated." He did not say what the slogans were; he left it to us to go and read them. The assembly was then dismissed without the headmaster saying anything. As we nervously walked towards our classrooms we now read the crudely scrawled words with black paint in Urdu. 'Headmaster is an infidel'. 'Headmaster is a Mirzai'. 'Headmaster should leave'.

So it was out in the open! Most of us knew that headmaster was a Mirzai. It was whispered among the students. I had also heard it mentioned at home; after all, our families were neighbours and good friends. My parents never made any comments, positive or negative, about the headmaster being of the Mirzai faith but I knew that some Muslims did not like Mirzais.

Mirzai was, and is, a derogatory term for people who call themselves Ahmadis. They belong to the Ahmadiyyaa movement whose founder, Mirza Ghulam Ahmad, was born in Northern India in 1835. When Ahmad was forty, he claimed that he was receiving revelations from Allah telling him that he was the Mahdi, the Messiah promised to the Muslims, and that his advent was in fulfillment of the various prophecies in Islam. Ahmad was a good organizer and soon his following increased substantially, though mainline Muslims disliked him, calling him a heretic. But as India was still under British rule, Mirza Ghulam Ahmad was free to teach what he liked. After the creation of Pakistan, things changed, and the hard-line *mullahs* were emboldened, demanding action against the infidel Ahmadis.

When I came home that evening I told my family what had happened at school. My father was not surprised. He had already heard that Maulvi Tamizuddin had talked against Mirzais in his Friday sermons and had called them *kafir*. I was told to keep my mouth shut and not to mix with students who talked against the headmaster.

The slogans were washed off the walls and were never repeated while I attended the school. There was little doubt that the Maulvi Sahib had incited some young people to write the slogans. This time he had gone too far, at least for the time being. Introducing *purdah* in girls' school and threatening to stop construction of a cinema was one thing, but instigating ethnic trouble was something which the authorities could not condone

I had almost forgotten this incident until 1975 when I was living in Canada as a landed immigrant. My Pakistani passport had expired and I was not yet eligible for the Canadian passport, so I called the Pakistani Embassy in Ottawa for an application for a new passport. The application asked for the applicant's religion, and when I put down "Muslim," it asked me to sign the following statement:

I am Muslim and believe in the absolute and
unqualified finality of the prophethood of Muhammad
(peace be upon him) the last of the prophets.

I do not recognize any person who claims to be a prophet
in any sense of the word or of any description whatsoever
after Muhammad (peace be upon him), or recognize such a
claimant as prophet or a religious reformer as a Muslim.

I consider Mirza Gulam Ahmad Quadiani to be an imposter
nabi and also consider his followers, whether belonging
to the Lahori or Quadiani group, to be non-Muslim.

It did not take me long to find out what had happened after I left Pakistan. Serious riots against Ahmadis had broken out in Pakistan in 1974. The government of Zulifqar Ali Bhutto, fearing complete breakdown of law and order, had passed an amendment to the Pakistan's constitution, which legally declared the Ahmadis to be non-Muslims.

In disgust I threw the application on the floor. It was outrageous, I said, that a government should force some Muslims to call themselves non-Muslim and label them so in their passports. I knew I should do something about it; raise my voice against this travesty, write to newspapers. But I was no different from my father — be nice and do nothing and things will work out. And my father was terminally ill in Pakistan. I had to go. Reluctantly, I picked the application from the floor and signed the declaration.

8

A new subject was introduced in our school curriculum, *Islamiyat*. This was one more step towards burnishing our Muslim credentials. Master Abdul Rashid was hired to teach *Islamiyat*. Master Rashid was not a qualified teacher; it was enough that he was well-versed in the Quran and *Hadith*. It would have been useful if he had taught us the history of Islam; there was so much that we could have learned. There are superb examples of Islamic art and architecture. For centuries Islam was the most tolerant religion; Jews expelled from Spain found refuge in the Muslim countries of North Africa, Turkey and Iran. Muslim scholars preserved the great writings of Greek philosophers and scientists during the Europe's Dark Ages. But Master Rashid confined his teaching to Quran and *Hadith*. Muslims rarely read Quran in their own language. It is almost always read in the original Arabic which only Arabic-speaking people can understand. Certainly there has never been any question of saying the mandatory five prayers in any language but Arabic. To his credit, Master Rashid did read to us the Urdu translation of Quran, but the Quranic verses are often directed at particular events in the Prophet's life, and are meaningless unless the context is explained. As Master Rashid rarely ventured into the background of the verses, if indeed he knew the background, they really meant little.

After a few months, Master Rashid decided that he did not have enough time in school to do a good job of teaching *Islamiyat*. He consequently suggested that students who did not have to rush home could meet with him after school in his house which was in a *muhalla* very near the school. Most of the students came from villages and could not stay after school; they had jobs to do at home. Only two or three of us, who lived close by, offered to stay. Master Rashid lived alone. As there were no chairs, we sat on a *durrie* spread on the floor. Away from school, Master Rashid felt free to talk of his own views on different aspects of Islam. He was a Wahabbi, he told us. I had vaguely heard of Wahabbis before, but Master Rashid said that it was simply being a true Muslim. Muhammad ibn Abd-al-Wahhab, an eighteenth-century scholar from what is known today as Saudi Arabia, was an ultraconservative Muslim who assisted the House of Saud in defeating their opponents and establishing the Saudi dynasty. In return, the Saudis promised to support the Wahabbi brand of Islam forever. In those days the Wahabbis were few and far between in Pakistan and were looked upon by others as a fringe group of no great importance. The oil money, which was to massively finance the Wahabbi movement, was yet to come.

"The problem with Muslims is that they do not practice their religion diligently," Master Rashid said. "That is why we are so far behind the western world. When we were true Muslims, we were the greatest power in the world. Remember Tariq? When he crossed the Strait of Gibraltar he burnt his boats so that, if defeated, he would not have the option of going back. He conquered Spain and almost conquered the whole of Europe. That is what we were then, and look what we are now." I doubt if Master Rashid had even been to Lahore but he took great delight in painting a stark picture of the West's decadence. The symbol of decadence was always the same: sexual freedom. Nothing, but nothing, was more abhorrent to him than girls losing their virginity before marriage or men and women cavorting in public.

Being a Wahabbi, Master Rashid was not well-disposed toward the Shias. There was a substantial Shia minority in town. They had their own prayer house which they called Immambara. I was familiar with the Shias because of the annual self-inflicted injuries at Muharram which my father had to treat in the hospital. The tenth day of the month of Muharram, called Ashura, is the anniversary of the death of Husain, Prophet Muhammad's grandson, who was killed at Karbala in the modern-day Iraq. The Prophet had died rather suddenly and left no instructions for succession. Within hours of his death, dissention broke out among his followers, between those who wanted to keep the succession (the caliphate) within the prophet's family, and those who favoured a wider franchise. The latter won and were called the Sunnis. The former, the Shias, are still smarting from humiliation. Almost fifty years after Prophet's death, friends of Husain convinced him that he should stake the claim once again to the caliphate. Husain consequently marched against the reigning caliph in Bagdad at the head of a ragtag band of followers, including women and children. They were no match for the caliph's soldiers who first cut off their water supply in the intense heat and then killed them in battle. On Ashura, Shias carry *tazias* and parade through the streets beating, excoriating, and flagellating themselves. At the height of their frenzy some mourners hurt themselves seriously and have to be carried to the hospital. My father was always expected to be ready at the hospital to receive the injured. Occasionally, a Sunni would hurl a taunt at the mourners and the resulting fight would add more casualties. It was a tense day and police were always deployed along the procession route.

One day Master Rashid suggested that I stay a little longer at his home. It was the month of Ramadan. "You don't have far to go. Why don't you stay and break fast with me." I told him that I was not fasting. "It does not matter. We can still eat together," he said. So I stayed and at the fast-breaking time Master Rashid brought out a small bowl of dates. "The Prophet always broke his fast with dates. It is a *sunnat*." Master Rashid, I thought, was getting excessively friendly. Was he just being kind or was there more to it? I did not like the way he had dismissed the other students and kept me there. My parents had always warned me of strangers offering friendship, and I was supposed to be on the lookout for it. "I have to go Masterji," I said a little later. "My family will be worried," which was true as I rarely came home late. Master Rashid tried to persuade me to stay longer but he did not actively stop me as I picked up my *basta* and left. I was confused as I came home. "Is it safe to go to Master Rashid's house? If not, what should I do?" I kept asking myself. I did not want to tell my parents. After all, if I told my father he might embarrass me by complaining to the headmaster. I did not think the headmaster even knew about these extra sessions of *Islamiyat*. I decided that I was going to tell no one but make an excuse to Master Rashid the following day, and stop going to his house. I felt nervous, alone and depressed. Why did I have to make these decisions on my own? But there was no one to turn to. The following day, I told Master Rashid that I could no longer come to his house after school as I had to help my mother milk the buffalo. I felt such relief when Master Rashid accepted my excuse by nodding his head.

9

Unmistakable changes in manners, dress and customs were taking place and they would intensify in the years to come. Adult men stopped wearing shorts as legs had to be covered. There was a time before 1947 when my father even went to work in long shorts in hot summer months. There were fewer and fewer women in the bazaar now and I never saw one in a sari which was considered a Hindu garment. The Hindu greeting of *namaste* was only a memory now except in the Indian movies which were soon banned anyway. The Sikh greeting of *sat sri akal* was a blasphemy. The liquor shops all over the country were closing down, first by threat, and then by legislation. Hindu and Sikh street names were eliminated and the streets were renamed after the great Muslim heroes. Unfortunately, the conflict over Kashmir accelerated the anti-India (read anti-Hindu) feelings. Soon, Hindu and Sikh culture will only be a remote memory, confined to those diminishing few who could remember pre-1947 India.

The exuberant fun of a multicultural society was replaced by a dull grey monotony, oppressive like the summer heat.

10

I cannot say that I was happy at home or at school. Outside the school I did not mix with other boys. Rafiq had gone away to the university in the autumn of 1947 and I saw little of him. My two sisters were home but were older and did not provide the company I needed. Hamida did all the cooking as my mother was often depressed and in poor health. The only staff at the hospital was my father's two *compounders* and a nurse. They did not have children of my age, and I was not allowed to play with servants' children, who did not go to school and were not considered by my father to be suitable company. My father was not elitist but he believed that I should only socialize with boys who were attending the school. He knew that few, if any, boys in Toba Tek Singh were going beyond high school, and he was determined that I should have a good education. It was not easy for me to invite friends to my house as I could not take them inside. We were now grown-up boys and not allowed to enter other homes where there were women. Most houses did not have separate rooms to entertain men, so if I did invite a friend we just had to sit or stand outside the house. As we had no radio or gramophone at home, I learned to keep my own company, and the company of books.

I suffered from loneliness at school, too. As I said before, almost all the students in school came from poor surrounding villages. I was the odd boy in the class. I had better clothes and more of them. Not that I was model of fashion. My clothes were sewn by my mother who had acquired a new Singer sewing machine; her old Pfaff was left behind in India. And my clothes were always clean. Other students, who rarely had a change of clothes, treated me with resentment and constantly taunted me. The only friend I had was Abdulla who was one of the few who was interested in school work, and worked hard at it. He came from a fairly distant village and had a long walk to school. I never visited his village. Like me, he did not like the rough and tumble, and he never taunted me.

My travails in school were aggravated by the teachers who appeared not to have any understanding of boys' psychology. I was routinely appointed the class monitor as I always had the highest marks. Being class monitor was a job I hated but could not refuse. After all, it was supposed to be an honour! Being monitor, I sat in front of the class, near the teacher. The monitor was expected to clean the chalk board after every class with a dirty rag, but it was the other jobs which made my life miserable. I was, for example, responsible for helping the teacher punish students for disobedience or for not doing their homework. There were two kinds of punishments. One was caning and the other was *kan pakrow*. There were never enough canes in the school, and the teacher needing one would ask the monitor to go out and fashion one from a tree branch. '*Kan pakrow*' means 'catch your ears'. The student, so punished, had to squat, put his arms under his legs and catch his ears while keeping his bottom raised. It is a very uncomfortable position to begin with and becomes excruciatingly painful within a few minutes. Your legs begin to tremble and sweat pours from your face. You instinctively lower your bum to ease pressure on your legs. Here is where the class monitor came in. He stood behind the victims and prodded their bottoms with his foot when the bottoms drooped. Occasionally, the teacher, seeing the bottoms drooping, would interrupt his lesson and give a couple of lashings to each bum with his cane. You can understand why the boys hated me for doing this job. Often, the boy so punished just waited till the end of the day to get even with me.

One boy who really took a dislike to me was Fazal. He was tall, strong and cruel, an archetypal bully. I was told that his well-to-do family was feared by all in his village. His dislike for me started one day when he was sentenced to *kan pakrow* for not doing his homework, and I was asked to stand behind him and make sure he kept his bottom up. After school, he waylaid me as I was walking home, threw me on the ground, kicked me, and walked away. From then on he did it often to me, and other boys watched it with glee. What could I do? As I said earlier, complaining was likely to make matters worse. I just had to put up with it.

At noon we had a one-hour recess. Most boys brought something to eat, usually a couple of *chapatis* with pickle. As I lived so near the school, I went home for lunch. One day my mother decided that I needed something for midmornings. She started sending a servant with a small jug of milk. The servant would stand just outside the classroom door. As one period finished and before the teacher arrived for the next period, the servant would wave to me to come out and drink my milk. This gave yet another reason for the boys to be mad at me. One day, Fazal grabbed the milk from the servant and drank it himself. The servant was taken aback but I asked the servant not to tell my parents and pretended to the servant that Fazal was doing it with my consent. I would rather that Fazal drank my milk, if it made him a little kinder to me. Actually, it made no difference.

11

Grade 10 was my last year in school. It was the toughest. The provincial matriculation examination which we all took at the end of grade 10 determined whether we could get admission to the university. I knew that in my class nobody else had any plan to go to the university. They were all going to finish their school and get on with their jobs in the villages. For me, university was everything. I could not imagine doing anything else. My parents expected it. The problem was that I attended a small town school with terrible standards, and now I was going to compete with all the students in the province and there were many better schools, some private, in the big cities. Our teachers often told us that our chances of competing with other students were bleak. "You may be good in your class here," a teacher once told me contemptuously. "But compared to students in the big cities you are nothing." Notwithstanding the relentless taunting from the students and occasional physical abuse from Fazal, I plodded on, though more and more I was wont to retreat in the garden of my imagination, surrounded by high walls. From the society around me, with its lies, deceit, and hypocrisy, I wanted nothing; neither its honey nor its sting.

A month before the exams, something happened which shook my confidence even further. We were handed out role numbers according to which we were going to be seated in the examination hall. To my surprise I found that Fazal was going to be sitting next to me. That in itself was not a big thing. He could not abuse me in the examination hall in the presence of invigilators. It was something, mentioned by another boy, which took me by surprise. "Look, Zahir, do you know why Fazal has maneuvered to sit next to you?"

"No, I don't."

"You see, our answer books go to different teachers in the province; they are not marked locally. Being close in role numbers, your and Fazal's answer books will most probably go to the same teacher. Fazal's family has connections and they can find out where the answer books have gone. They will then contact that teacher and bribe him to exchange the covers of the answer books. Fazal will get your marks!"

I was shocked when this was suggested to me. Now I had to do something. I could not take it anymore as this was now a matter of life and death for me. I went home and told my father what I had heard. Though he was not convinced, he could see the logic behind it. With rampant corruption and abysmally poor teacher salaries, this kind of thing had probably happened before. My father went to see the headmaster. The headmaster did not believe the story. "Students do ask their teachers, when they submit their names for exams, to be seated next to clever students," he said. "They do this in the hope that they may be able to whisper answers to each other when the invigilator is not nearby. But swapping the answer books? Frankly, I have never heard of it and don't believe things have become this bad." My father came home and tried to put my worries to rest, but I knew I was not going to be completely reassured until the results were out.

The last day in our school the grades 6 to 9 gave us a farewell party as we sat under the trees. It was already late spring and very hot. That was the last day of my school. The school had not been easy, but it was over.

After the exams I had nothing to do but wait a few weeks for the results. As usual, I read whatever was available. My father had brought home a used copy of *War and Peace*; 'the greatest novel ever written', its cover said.

A few weeks later, the results of the provincial matriculation examination were published in all the daily newspapers. I had achieved a stunning success. Out of thousands of students in the Punjab I was in the top ten. Never in our town had any student done so well. The headmaster himself came to congratulate my father. My father who rarely showed any emotion put his arms around me; this was only the second time he did so, the first time was in Jalandhar after the train massacre. Now when I walked down the bazaar, people came up to me and shook my hand.

Fazal had failed the exams; my fear of his scheme had been unfounded.

I could now apply for all kinds of grants and scholarships. It was the end of my days in Toba Tek Singh.

12

I went back to Toba Tek Singh in 1970 when I was living in the US. I no longer knew anyone there. My parents had left to live with Rafiq in Lahore. It was a hot summer day as I walked from the train station to the school, stopping under an occasional tree to cool down. The school was closed for the summer vacation. The gate was padlocked but I could look through the gate. It looked more run-down than I had imagined, but whether it had really deteriorated or whether in all those years I had embellished its image in my memory, I know not. I do know from experience that poor countries look poorer on a revisit, after you have spent time in the West. I went to the bazaar, to the old bookshop, which was still there. I wanted to find out if any of my classmates was in town.

After asking around, I found one. It was Saeed whom I remembered well. He was a good boy with whom I got along well in school. He now ran Saeed Photography Studio near the centre of the bazaar. It was just a one-room shop. We recognized each other. Saeed was very glad to see me and embraced me warmly. "I make reasonable living," he said. "Mostly I photograph children whom the proud parents bring, but I also take photos for passports. A lot of people are going to the Gulf to work, and need passports." We were sitting on a bench, drinking *chai*, outside his studio. I asked after various people. Abdulla, he said, had joined the army. Many young people in the villages had done so, as Pakistan, with American military aid, was expanding its army. He thought Abdullah was in the air force, perhaps a pilot.

"Do you remember Master Rashid?" I asked.

"Oh, yes. Master Rashid," Saeed said, laughing quietly. "He got into major trouble. He was caught buggering some of his students whom he had invited to his house. The local magistrate decided to give him the more traditional punishment instead of usual prison term. A garland of old shoes was put around his neck. His face was smeared with black paint and he was made to sit on a donkey, facing backwards, with a sign describing his offence hanging around his neck as he was paraded through the bazaar. I saw it all myself. He left town soon after."

I was not surprised, just saddened. I felt sorry for Master Rashid. He was a kind and generous person who wanted to be a good Muslim and a good Wahabbi. Wahabbi or not, he had his hormones, which I suppose got the better of him. How humiliating it must have been; one minute a schoolmaster, the next paraded through the bazaar in disgrace!

"Do you remember a boy named Fazal?" I asked.

"Don't you know?" Saeed looked at me with surprise.

"Know what?" I said.

"Don't you know what happened to Fazal?" Saeed said again.

"No. I have been out of the country all these years, you see. What happened to him?"

"Well, you see, he was hanged," Saeed said.

"Hanged?" I was stunned.

"Yes. Do you remember how aggressive and short-tempered he used to be? He got into a fight in his village and killed a man with a knife."

We fell silent for a while and then, suddenly, I was visited by a thought so ignoble that I was ashamed to admit it. I was glad that Fazal was hanged.

13

In the Pakistan Pavilion of the 1986 World Exposition at Vancouver there was an exhibit of Pakistan's history. It started with the Indus Civilization of Harappa and Mohenjo-Daro (2000 BCE) and then jumped to the conquest of Sind by Muhammad bin Qasim (711 CE). It then described the Muslim rule in India, and jumped again to the establishment of Pakistan in 1947.

Walking with me, an elderly British visitor remarked, "My father was an engineer who spent his working life in India. I know he supervised construction of a number of important dams in what is now Pakistan. Looking at this exhibition it would appear that the British never had any connection with Pakistan."

"Same for the Hindus and Sikhs," I added. "No mention of them either. After all, Hindus ruled that area for centuries before the Muslims arrived."

"Why is that, you think?" asked the Englishman.

I did not know what to say. "It is a long story," I finally said, as we parted company.

NOTES

Prologue

1. *Jarnaili sarak,* The Grand Trunk Road, often abbreviated as the "GTRoad" connects Calcutta with Peshawar. Its origins are lost in history but its current route was marked by Sher Shah Suri (1486-1545). Later Indian rulers planted trees along the road and built caravanserais. British resurfaced it. See: Harvey Arden, "Searching for India: Along the Grand Trunk Road", *National Geographic* Vol.177, No. 5 (May 1990), 118-38. Anthony Waller, *Days and Nights on the Grand Trunk Road: Calcutta to Khyber,* New York: Marlowe & Company, 1997.

2. Guru Gobind Singh (1666-1708) was the tenth and last guru of the Sikhs. He founded *Khalsa,* the militant Sikh order with its five symbols of unshorn hair, comb, bracelet, special underwear, and a sword. Gobind Singh gave a heavily aggressive interpretation to the first Guru Nanak's entirely peaceful teachings. Sikhism, consequently, has

retained its dual personality of unmatched hospitality with uncommon violence.

3. My wife's mother grew up as a Protestant in a Catholic village in Ireland. From what I heard from her, I can say that there was greater camaraderie between the Hindu, Muslim and Sikh children in pre-1947 Punjab than between the Protestant and Catholic children of Ireland.

4. On more recent travels on the subcontinent I now see many people sitting on the ground in the morning with bottles of water, though Gandhi's sensible advice to take a trowel to dig a hole to bury one's excrement never became popular.

5. Though the Indian and Pakistani leaders and writers have routinely made the Jallianwalla massacre a symbol of British brutality, they have shed few tears over the murder of 50,000 Kashmiris and over one million Bengalis killed by the Indian and Pakistani military respectively. They too were fighting for independence.

6. Udham Singh is considered a martyr by most Indians. In July 1974, his remains were exhumed and repatriated to India at the request of Indira Gandhi. A district in Northern India has been named after him.

7. The Unionist Party was a pro-British political party which promoted continued allegiance to the Crown. Its power base was in Punjab and it was led by secular wealthy landowners.

8. Theosophy is a doctrine of religious philosophy and metaphysics originating with Helena Petrovna Blavatsky (1831-1891). It holds that each religion has a portion of the truth. See www.theosophy.com

9. Timur (Tamerlane of English literature) was locally nicknamed Timurlung (Timur, the lame) because of his

limping gait. His horrific mass murder of civilians in Delhi became legendary, and Indian mothers used to discipline their children by invoking his name. Mughals were his descendents.

10. This promise was made by Lord Minto, Viceroy of India, in 1906 to a delegation of prominent Muslims, headed by the Agha Khan.

11. Thugs were originally members of a semi-religious Indian cult of *Thugee*, people who engaged in the multiple murder and robbery of travelers; it was associated with the followers of the Hindu Goddess Kali. Thugs killed over one million unsuspecting travellers by strangling them with a special piece of cloth called the *rumal*. They were finally eliminated by the British in 1830 under the direction of William Sleeman. See Philip Meadows Taylor, *Confessions of a Thug* (1839), Oxford University Press, 1986. John Masters, *The Deceivers*, New York: Carroll & Graf, 1988.

12. *The Civil & Military Gazette*, published in Lahore, was the well-known English newspaper of the time. From 1882 to 1887 Rudyard Kipling served as its sub-editor. The newspaper closed its doors in 1963 after almost one hundred years of publication.

13. Later that year, when Headmaster Bhalla heard of the terrible calamity which had befallen our family, he wrote a letter of deep sorrow to my father in Pakistan.

14. Sikhs did this again in 1984 under Jarnail Singh Bhindranwale, which resulted in the storming of the Golden Temple by the Indian Army. This time, unlike in 1947, the Indian Army took strong, decisive action.

15. We met Dr. Husain many months later in Pakistan. My father's blunder for not opting for Pakistan was by then too obvious to be mentioned.

The Catastrophe

1. The term *bogie* is universally used for a carriage or compartment of a train in India. In the rest of this book I have used the term carriage or compartment.

2. Years later, a Muslim in Pakistan told me, "I was a soldier in 1947 guarding a train of Muslim refugees travelling to Pakistan. Near Amritsar, I saw two Sikhs standing near the train tracks talking and laughing. I suddenly lost my cool, raised my rifle and shot them both from the moving train."

3. A Pakistani doctor told me a similar story, "In 1947 I was in charge of a hospital in Pakistan. We were getting many wounded Sikhs. The problem was that as soon as they were discharged, they were waylaid outside the hospital and killed. When I objected, I was told by the Muslim *goondas* that if I kept them inside the hospital after treatment, they would enter the hospital and kill them in the wards."

Epilogue

1. Muslims were actually outnumbered three to one at Badr. The Battle of Badr has often been described by historians as one of the most important battles in the history of mankind. At the time, it was really a skirmish in the backwaters of Arabian Peninsula.

2. Abdul Malik (646-705CE), Umayyad caliph in Damascus, was a descendant of Abu Sufyan, one of Muhammad's bitterest enemies who later converted to Islam. Muhammad's descendents challenged Abu Sufyan's family for usurping the Caliphate, resulting in a prolonged and bloody fight which Muhammad's descendents lost.

The violent origins of early Islam were to leave a lasting legacy.

3. Serendip is the old Arab name for Siri Lanka. The term "serendipity" is derived from Serendip, featured in a tale, called *The Three Princes of Serendip* (1557). Whenever the princes travelled, they made discoveries, by accident, of things which they were not looking for.

4. The custom of sending the severed head of the enemy to the ruler is prehistoric. See Lawrence Keeley, *War Before Civilization,* Oxford: Oxford University Press, 1996. When Prophet Muhammad's grandson, Husain, was killed at Karbala, he was beheaded and his head taken to the Caliph Yazid bin Muawiyah at Damascus.

5. *Chach Nama* (Chronicles of Chach) was written by an Arab contemporary of Qasim. Chach was the father of King Dahar. The original Arabic text has been lost but its Persian translation by Ali bin Kufi in 1216 CE is extant and was translated into English by Mountstuart Elphinstone (1779-1859), Governor of Bombay.

6. Burying victims alive in a wall was not rare. Anarkali, a legendry slave-girl, was reportedly ordered to be buried alive in a wall by the Mughal emperor Akbar for daring to have an illicit relationship with his son. The legacy of Muhammad bin Qasim in Sind is a mixed one. Though he is lionized by Muslims in general and a new port near Karachi has been named after him, some Sindhis nevertheless consider Arab invasion an unfortunate event which destroyed much of the Sindhi culture.

7. None of these stories is true. The idols were made of stone and were solid, not hollow. The story of the Somnath gates had a dénouement in 1842 when the British-Indian forces, under orders from Lord Ellenborough, claimed to have brought the gates back to India. Alas, the gates were

found to be a clumsy forgery. The *Menat* was one of the three pre-Islamic Arab goddesses whose idols were kept in Kaaba. These goddesses appear in Salman Rushdie's *Satanic Verses,* New York: Viking, 1998. The Somnath temple was rebuilt by Hindus immediately after Indian independence

GLOSSARY

abaji: father.
acha bacha: good boy.
achkin: a long tight coat, traditionally worn by Muslims in North India.
achoot: untouchable.
Akali Dal: literary, "eternal cloud." A militant Sikh movement.
Akhand Bharat: Undivided India, dominated by the Hindus.
Allah o Akbar: God is Great.
Allama Mashriqi: the Wise man of the East.
angrez: British.
angrezi log: British people.
angrezi raj: British rule.
arthi: broker.
badmash: ruffian.
bahishti: water- carrier.
bania: member of a Hindu merchant class, known for sharp business practices.
bara baje: midday.
bara paramatma: the big God.
basta: satchel.
basti: neighbourhood, usually poor.

belcha: spade.
ber: a tropical fruit.
bhai: brother, friend.
bhang: marijuana.
bindi: mark on the forehead often made by Hindus.
bohr: banyan.
bola: deaf.
burqa: a piece of clothing that covers a woman from head to foot with an opening for the eyes.
butprust: idol-worshiper.
butshikan: idol-breaker.
chai: tea.
chamar: one of the many classes of untouchables.
charpoy: Indian string-bed.
chaprasi: peon.
chapati: Unleavened flat bread of Northern India.
chillum: the container on the top of a *hookah* containing tobacco and burning coal.
chota paramatma: the little God.
cho: a torrent in the foothills of Punjab which is dry most of the year except in the rainy season.
chulla: Indian indoor hearth.
compounder: a compounding-dispenser. In those days most medicines were locally mixed in the hospital dispensary.
Congresswalla: a member of Congress Party.
dacoit: robber.
dada: paternal grandfather.
dal: lentils.
dalia: porridge made from cracked-wheat.
dhaba: a modest roadside eating place.
dhoti: A loincloth worn by Hindu men in India.
diwa: a small earthen cup holding vegetable oil and a cotton wick, used in Indian villages for lighting.
doab: Persian word meaning two waters but used in Punjab to describe newly irrigated land after building of river dams by the British.
dopatta: loose, long head covering.

dungar: animals.
durrie: a thick, woven cotton fabric.
Flit Gun: brand name insecticide sprayer.
gada: bullock-cart.
gal khotu: literally, "throat strangler". It was the local name for post-First World War Spanish flu.
goonda: a common criminal.
gulab jamin: an Indian sweet.
gurdwara: Sikh house of worship.
Hadith: a traditional account of things said or done by Muhammad or his companions.
hafiz: a term used by Muslims for people who have completely memorized the Quran
Hajar al Aswad: the sacred stone in the wall of Kaaba in Mecca.
hakim: a physician, usually a Muslim, and usually practicing herbal medicine.
hartal: strike, with shutting down of shops and withdrawal of civil services.
haveli: a private residence with a courtyard.
hilal: meat of the animal who is killed by slitting of throat and consequent blood-letting.
Hindu Mahasabha: a Hindu nationalist organization, founded in 1915 by V.D. Savarkar.
Hindu-Muslim bhai bhai: Hindus and Muslims are brothers.
hookah: an Eastern smoking pipe designed with a long tube passing through an urn of water that cools the smoke as it is drawn through.
houri: One of the beautiful virgins of the Muslim paradise.
hookahbardar: the servant with sole responsibility of looking after his master's *hookah*.
Islamiyat: study of Islam.
Jai Hind: Hail to India.
jaloose: public procession.
jalsa: public assembly.
Jama Masjid: the great mosque at Delhi, built by Emperor Shah Jahan in 1656 AD.

jaman: a tropical fruit.
Jang-e-Azadi: Battle of Independence.
jatha: a gang, usually armed, of Sikhs.
Kaaba: Islam's holiest site in Mecca.
kabristan: graveyard.
kacha: made of mud, as opposed to *pacca* which is made of kiln-dried bricks.
kafir: infidel.
kafla: caravan.
kala pani: literally, "black water" but the term was used for Andaman Islands where some serious criminals were sent for life.
kalma: Muslim oath of faith.
karakul cap: also called Jinnah cap, made of sheep fur.
keriana: groceries.
kesai: butcher.
khandaq: trench.
Khizry tattoo hai hai: Down with Khizr, the (British) mule.
kirpan: a sword traditionally carried by Sikhs. In those days many Sikhs carried full-sized swords.
kulla: a cap around which a turban is wound.
Laat Sahib: literally, "the big boss". The term was often used for Viceroy or for Provincial Governors.
lathi: long stick, usually metal-tipped.
lathi charge: use of *lathis* by police to disperse unlawful crowds.
lingam: the male sexual organ. It is a symbol for the worship of the Hindu deity Shiva.
Lokamanya: literally, "Revered by the People", the title given to Hindu nationalist leader Bal Gangadhar Tilak.
maan de bete: children of our mother.
mader chod: mother-fucker.
malka: empress.
Malka e Hind: Empress of India, a title first assumed by Queen Victoria.
manchod: mother-fucker.
mashk: a container made of goatskin to carry water.

mathai: Indian sweets.
maulvi: a Muslim cleric.
mehtar: member of a low Hindu caste, with duties of sweeping and cleaning toilets.
mochi: cobbler.
Mooslay or Moosla: derogatory terms for a Muslim.
muhalla: neighbourhood.
mullah: a Muslim cleric.
munshi: low-level clerk. Here it means a teacher of Urdu.
murdabad: literally "death to ---" but may imply 'down with---."
murghi: chicken.
murid: follower of a Sufi *pir*.
Mussalman murdabad: death to Muslims.
nabi: prophet.
namaste: The Hindu greetings with hands pressed together and held near the heart and the head bowed.
nana: maternal grandfather.
nani: maternal grandmother.
Nankana Sahib: birthplace of Guru Nanak, founder of Sikh religion.
naqar: public announcement by a *naqari*.
naqari: town-crier.
nawab: an important landowner in India.
pacca: made of kiln-dried bricks, as opposed to *kacha* which is made of mud.
pahara: multiplication table.
Pakistan murdabad: Death to Pakistan.
Pakistan zindabad: Long live Pakistan.
pan: betel leaf mixed with various spices.
paramatma: a Hindu term for God, almost identical to the tern *Bhagwan*.
patang: kite.
peshwa: the office of Chief Minister among the Marathas.
pir: a pious man among the Sufis who acts as a kind of intermediary between man and God.
pugree: turban.

purdah: a system to keep women secluded at home. Also, to keep women's body covered in public.
Quaid-e-Azam: literally, "The Great Leader", the title given to Muhammad Ali Jinnah by his followers.
qari: a Muslim religious instructor.
raj kare ga Khalsa: Sikhs will rule.
Ram Ram mantra: repetitive use of the word "Ram" as a Hindu devotional custom.
roti: chapati.
sahib log: important people. The term was usually, though not exclusively, used for the British.
salam, kaya hal he: hello, how are you?
samraj: ruler.
sat sri akal: Sikh greeting, originally part of a war cry.
satyagraha: peaceful agitation, in principle at least.
sepoy: from Persian word *sipahi*, meaning a soldier.
Serendip: Arab name for Siri Lanka.
shalwar-kamiz: : Punjabi loose shirt and baggy trousers.
shirab: alcohol.
shorba: broth.
sone ki chiria: literally "the golden sparrow." The term is often used to describe a very rich country.
Sufi: member of Sufi faith, a mystical branch of Islam.
sunnat: something which is not mandatory but desirable for a Muslim to do because Prophet Muhammad was in the habit of doing it.
suttee: self-immolation of a wife on her husband's funeral pyre.
takht ya takhta: throne or funeral pyre.
takhti: specially made plank of wood to write on.
tati: lavatory.
tattoo: mule.
taxiwalla: taxi driver.
tazia: replica of the tomb of Husain, grandson of Prophet Muhammad.
Tehrik-e-khaksar: Movement of the People.
thana: police station.

thanidar: head constable, in charge of a small police station.
tiddydul: locust cloud.
tikka: mark on the forehead often made by Hindus.
Toady Party murdabad: Down with Toady Party.
tonga: horse-drawn cart.
turra: crest of a turban.
wazir-e-azam: the Grand Vizier.
zakat: Islamic system of tithing and alms.

SELECTED READING

Bristow, R.C.B. 1974. *Memories of the British Raj.* London: Johnson.

French, Patrick. 1997. *Liberty or Death.* London: HarperCollins.

Hibbert, Christopher.1978. *Indian Mutiny.* London: Allen Lane

Moon, Penderel. 1961. *Divide and Quit. An Eyewitness Account of the Partition of India.* London: Chatto and Windus.

Mosley, Leonard. 1961. *The Last Days of the British Raj.* London: Weidenfeld and Nicholson

Singh, Khushwant. 1956. *Train to Pakistan.* New York: Grove Press.

Tuker, Francis.1950. *While Memory Serves.* London: Cassell.

Wolpert, Stanley. 1984. *Jinnah of Pakistan.* Oxford: Oxford University Press.

Wolpert, Stanley. 1991. *Tilak and Gokhale.* Oxford: Oxford University Press.

Wolpert, Stanley. 1996. *Nehru.* Oxford: Oxford University Press.

LaVergne, TN USA
10 March 2011
219553LV00004B/8/P